Praise for
Kid on the Go!

In *Kid on the Go!*, memoirist Neill McKee takes us back to his childhood where he first discovers the strange features of his hometown of Elmira, Ontario, Canada. He shares his own views of the world with the eyes of a child and of the adult that he is now. Enriched with details, including clever artwork by McKee himself, along with family photographs, this memoir will take you on a journey through the author's past. Both funny and insightful, clever and thought-provoking, it's a book you don't want to miss.

—NICOLE PYLES, WRITER,
PORTLAND, OREGON, USA WORLDOFMYIMAGINATION.COM

Kid on the Go! is an honest, engaging, and sometimes humorous story that contains just the right amount of detail. It's a thought-provoking memoir of childhood and youth that drew me right in. McKee is an expert storyteller with a great sense of humor.

—CRYSTAL OTTO, BOOK BLOGGER AND REVIEWER,
REEDSVILLE, WISCONSIN, USA

In *Kid on the Go!*, Neill McKee describes his growing up in Elmira, Ontario, and his life and education in Ontario and Alberta, from the late 1940s up to the time he departed to teach in Borneo, in 1968. He presents a vivid picture of his hometown as he experienced it, often indicating his later understanding, while including drawings from a child's and youthful viewpoint, and many photographs. He gives us well-told accounts of the pollution in the town, but tells humorous stories about his family, his teachers, his adolescent misadventures, his encounters with the 1960s counter-culture, and his developing intellectual interests. The book concludes with a moving postscript, "Closing the Circle," where he describes Elmira as it is today, and speaks of the deaths of his parents. *Kid on the Go!* tells us what it was really like to grow up in Canada during that era.

—**BILL EXLEY**, RETIRED ENGLISH TEACHER, LONDON, ONTARIO, CANADA

Neill McKee's new book, *Kid on the Go!*, reminds us of the importance of storytelling, for as author Brian McLaren says, "It is through storytelling that we are given direction, values, vision and inspiration." The description of McKee's childhood could be ours, and that is why this book is important. He has sought to understand what made him the adult who would eventually visit and work in over 80 countries. But I think this memoir is more than about venturing out in a geographical sense. It is about seeking new experiences, venturing out in a social sense, forming and valuing relationships with the stranger, the marginalized, and those who think differently. It is all told with a gentle sense of humour and delightful drawings.

—**BRUCE WILLIAMSON**, ALSO NOW A SENIOR "KID ON THE GO," PORT HOPE, ONTARIO, CANADA

Neill McKee has the ability to explain life's experiences in a way I can easily relate to. When I read about McKee's early adventures and the lessons he learned, I experienced a lot of reborn fun, joy and memories of the projects my friends and I created, with nothing but imagination and inspiration. They were just like what McKee writes about with his classic style and humor.

—CHARLES MANN ROLISON, RETIRED,
ALBUQUERQUE, NEW MEXICO, USA

While this saga is an amusing trip down memory lane, it is also an intense drama of an unfolding life. On the amusing side we are entertained with 'tongue-in-cheek' humor as Neill McKee learns the ways of the world from "older and wiser" cousins and friends. But on a more serious side, the author invites us on a journey that will cause us to reflect on the building blocks of our own adult lives. McKee's formative years were spent in a society that knew little diversity and where tolerance was limited to tolerating different interpretations of Christianity. In the last chapters and a postscript, we learn about the factors that led him to an international career, traveling to Africa, Asia, Latin America, the Caribbean, and living in seven diverse countries.

—KEN FREY ED. D., RETIRED MANAGEMENT CONSULTANT,
MILTON, ONTARIO, CANADA

Kid on the Go! does an impressive thing, it uses naive illustrations to tell an ever-evolving story of growth and maturation. Neill McKee covers his early life in the middle of the 20th century—kids exploring neighborhoods and creeks, and young emotions, in approachable prose and conversational storytelling. The illustrations that accompany these anecdotes are similarly plucky, sketchy, and approachable. You can feel the artist's youth pour through the sketchy lines. As young Neill matures, the content of his stories develop into exploring sexuality, physicality, and disillusionment. His prose gets more sophisticated too—we read about complicated emotions in more complicated syntaxes. But why I want to recommend this book, is that the drawings stay the same. Sure, he begins to draw more mature subjects: electroshock therapy, ugly cityscapes, racy cars and women, but the style still retains that childlike sketchiness and approachability. That juxtaposition is really captivating. So, I'd like to thank the author for summoning the bravery to both write *and* draw his story.

—**DAV YENDLER**, ILLUSTRATOR,
LOS ANGELES, CALIFORNIA, USA DAVYENDLER.COM

Neill McKee takes readers on a tour of how he began experiencing the world. People who grew up in small town North America in the 40s, 50s and early 60s, when kids had freedom to roam the countryside, exploring its side roads, creeks, rivers, and woods, will find themselves snickering and laughing out loud as memories of their own youth pour forth. This freedom to explore his immediate environment when young, without regulations and structure created by adults, leads Neill to explore, physically and intellectually, the wider world as he matures and takes the reader through his university days, with whimsical humour, and finally off to teach in Sabah, Malaysia, a job that eventually leads him to an international career. It's a great story by itself and a prequel to his first memoir, *Finding Myself in Borneo*. A good read and great job!

—**GWENDA MCCURDY**, AVID READER,
BRAMPTON ONTARIO, CANADA

Kid

on the

Go!

Kid

on the

Go!

Memoir of My Childhood and Youth

NBFS CREATIONS

ALBUQUERQUE, NEW MEXICO, USA

WWW.NEILLMCKEEAUTHOR.COM

KID ON THE GO!
By Neill McKee

NBFS CREATIONS LLC
Albuquerque, New Mexico, USA
www.neillmckeeauthor.com
© 2021 Neill McKee

Literary editor: Pamela Yenser, NM Book Editors, LLC
Copy editor and proofreader: Varsana Tikovsky
Book and cover designer: The Book Designers, bookdesigners.com
Illustrations: Neill McKee
Photo credits: Family sources and by the author

Publisher's Cataloging-in-Publication data

Names: McKee, Neill, 1945-, author.
Title: Kid on the go! memoir of my childhood and youth / Neill McKee.
Description: Albuquerque, NM: NBFS Creations LLC, 2021.
Identifiers: LCCN: 2021912984 | ISBN: 978-1-7329457-5-3 (paperback) | 978-1-7329457-6-0 (ebook)
Subjects: LCSH McKee, Neill. | McKee, Neill--Homes and haunts--Ontario--Elmira. | Ontario--Biography. | Ontario--Elmira--Biography. | Ontario--Elmira--History. | Factory and trade waste--Canada. | BISAC BIOGRAPHY & AUTOBIOGRAPHY / Personal Memoirs
Classification: LCC F1057. M35 2021| DDC 971.07/2092--dc23

*To my late parents, Russell and Alma McKee,
who gave me the time and space to wonder,
and wander far from home.*

Acknowledgments

I would like to thank those who are familiar with Elmira and gave me feedback on their own impressions of the time and place we shared, especially Bill Exley, Ruth Overy, Jeanette Panagapka, Ken Frey, and Bob Kavanagh. They provided concrete suggestions for improvements and/or checked facts. I also much appreciate the input, including photos, received from my siblings, especially from my brother Glen, who answered many questions I had on our joint boyhood escapades, jogging my memory. I recognize that what we recall of past events often varies.

I also appreciate Catharine Neill's help in sharing memories of her adopted brother-cousin Richard Neill. My wife, Elizabeth, and daughter, Ruth, as well as professional illustrator Dav Yendler, encouraged me to continue to draw the illustrations found in this book. I had not attempted any "artwork" since elementary school, and doubted my ability to work in this medium. I would also like to recognize the creative changes and suggestions made by Pamela Yenser, my literary editor, who guided me on structure, story development, voice, and language. Finally, I would like to thank all those who provided prepublication reviews in the preceding "Praise for Kid on the Go!"

"You can go other places, all right—you can live on the other side of the world, but you can't ever leave home."

—SUE MONK KIDD

"Snow and adolescence are the only problems that disappear if you ignore them long enough."

—EARL WILSON

"Everybody's youth is a dream, a form of chemical madness."

—F. SCOTT FITZGERALD

Contents

THAT'S ME, THE SHRIMP!

1

Odiferous Ontario Origins

I came into this world as the third child and second son of Russell and Alma McKee. My father stood only five-foot six and my mother was about an inch taller. They both had dark brown hair, his combed straight back and hers evenly rolled under in that plain 1940s style. He presented himself in a modest and shy manner, but had a good store of jokes and stories to repeat. Mom would often break out in a giggle at his punch lines, or at some funny memory of her own. This made her prettier, in my opinion.

I was born a few months after World War II ended, in Kitchener-Waterloo Hospital, about 13 miles (21 km) from my hometown, Elmira, Ontario. At the time, it was a town of about 3,000 people, located in the heavily populated part of Canada at the same latitude or farther south than 15 American states. When you mention this to most Americans, they just look at you with an expression that says, "Don't take me for an idiot. I know Canada's up North."

Dad had an acute sense of smell. He could sniff out anything that was "off," as he called it, and would be the first to point out in an authoritative voice, "It stinks like a skunk, a dead rat, or a rotting fish"—a tone he reserved for this sense only. Like him, I never had any nasal blockages. From my early days, I became aware of the foul smells all around me.

In Elmira, as I recall, the predominant wind from the west came loaded with the pungent stink from generous quantities of pig and cow manure, courtesy of the Mennonite farmers' fields on the west side of town. I noticed it most in spring and fall and longed for winter when all the fields would be frozen and blanketed in many feet of snow.

WESTERLY WIND FRAGRANCE

Shifting winds from the north brought no relief. The fields on that side of town were equally full of animal dung with an added "fragrance" from the slaughterhouse, which my brother Glen called "skunk factory." I never went inside but I can recall an old horse with an ugly hump on its back, pacing back and forth in the corral outside of skunk factory, waiting for its fate to be sealed—or should I say "glued"? I couldn't understand how this unfortunate beast could be reduced to glue, or why the light brown paste we used at school didn't stink.

Winds from the east proved to be more complex and beyond my childish understanding. By the time I was born, Elmira's Naugatuck Chemical factory, located on that side of town—once a branch of a Connecticut firm—had graduated from producing a substance used in World War II bombs, to turning out new rubber and plastic products. [Much later I learned from studying

EASTERLY WIND DAYS

3

the matter that Naugatuck also gave off clouds of acids, sulfates, and nitrates—noxious fumes few people could identify at the time. The factory's new outputs included particles of its latest products: an insecticide called DDT and two "miracle" herbicides—2,4-D, known as "Weed Bane" and the stronger 2,4,5-T, marketed as "Brush Bane." In the 1940s, Elmira was declared the "first weed-free town in Canada" due to a scheme of spraying all the lawns with discount herbicide from Naugatuck. High school students were even roped into the job.]

The chemical plant then stood, and still stands today, near the stately middle-class brick houses of Duke, Water (now called "Wyatt"), and Erb Streets. But its effects extended throughout most of the town, especially on easterly-wind days. Some residents reported, "It's great. You don't have to weed your garden. Weed Bane must be floating in the air." Sometimes doubters chimed in, "My tomatoes taste kind of odd. Don't yours?" But everyone liked the fact that their yards were almost mosquito-free due to the DDT.

Most days, Naugatuck's daily odorous outputs were enhanced with contributions from Read Brothers Fertilizers, located about a half-mile from the houses on Duke Street. Read Brothers added the aromas of nitrogen, potash, and phosphate to the town's air, which were hard to differentiate from Naugatuck's contributions, except by those with the most discerning noses.

I especially remember, as a boy, how all these eastside factory vapors mixed with the stench of decaying food, dead rats, and burning rubber tires coming from the town dump situated just to the south of Naugatuck. On easterly-wind days, I had to hold my breath a lot or cup my hands over my nose and mouth. My hands, though dirty from playing in all sorts of places, often smelled a little better than the air. They had a definite salty-sweet smell, especially with the addition of summer sweat.

The wind rarely blew from the south, but when it did, it carried puffs from rubber and plastic factories, and more acceptable whiffs from the breweries and distilleries located in the twin cities of Kitchener-Waterloo. My dad told me Kitchener used to be called "Berlin" before World War I, a sure sign hard-working, beer-drinking Germans populated the city.

Gradually, I memorized all these stink patterns. I didn't even have to wet my finger and stick it in the air to tell the direction of the wind. But on windless days, the town's smell caused a metallic taste in my mouth. I watched black flecks drifting down from the tall smokestacks of Link Belt Foundry in the center of Elmira. They clung to my clothes and flapped between the tiny hairs inside my nostrils. On some winter days, these dark speckles coated the snow and our clothes drying on Mom's clothesline, making her have to re-wash and re-hang.

I don't think my mother or her friends and neighbors minded washing their laundry over again. The black flecks were a sign of the post-war boom—new jobs and prosperity in our small town. Local residents and outside investors had added additional factories such as Martin's Feed Mills, which gave off a suffocating odor, causing me to hold my nose when I walked by; Bonnie's Chick Hatchery, which smelled like stale pee; Elmira Shirt and Overall Company, which I knew from its starchy fragrance; and Elmira Furniture, which thankfully produced the aroma of freshly cut wood, as did Beaver Lumber. I liked to walk by those places and breathe deeply. Likewise, I didn't have to pinch my nostrils when I entered the farm equipment business my father and his twin brother Gerald started in the mid-1940s. By then, they'd begun designing and making hay blowers in a small garage near the center of town, and their business took off from there. I actually liked the smell of shaping, welding, and grinding metal.

MCKEE BROTHERS' FIRST MACHINE SHOP

By the time I was five or six, I was allowed to roam our neighborhood with Glen. Most of the houses in Elmira already had indoor plumbing, but one nearby backyard usually reeked of fresh poop. At first Glen and I didn't know where this foul smell was coming from. Then one day, we discovered a large pen surrounded by chicken wire at the back of that neighbor's house. The ground inside looked all gooey and smelled awful, but we couldn't see any chickens in the enclosure. We debated over the origin of this guck for some time until, one day, we brought our older and wiser cousins David and Alec to the scene.

I asked, "What's this smelly mess?"

"Ostrich shit," David said like a know-it-all.

"But where are the ostriches?"

"They come out at night," Alec said.

"From where? I've got a storybook that says ostriches live in Africa."

David replied, "Africans sometimes bring them here."

I had never seen any Africans in town and I sure had not laid eyes on any ostriches. The only black people I'd ever seen lived in small ramshackle houses on the 3rd Concession, near our Uncle John's farm, 15 miles (24 km) to the northwest. My father, who was born there, told us stories about the history of the area. He said those people descended from African slaves who escaped from the United States about 100 years ago, using a secret underground railway. I didn't really understand how this could be possible because such a long tunnel, tall and wide enough for trains, would have been hard to build back then. All the same, the idea seemed pretty neat.

I asked David and Alec, "Do you think they come and go with their ostriches on the underground railway during the night?"

"Prob-ly," Alec said with a smirk. David and Alec knew so much more than we did because they had a whole shelf of comic books in their bedroom, including my favorite one, *Archie*. Sometimes, they'd let Glen and me look at them and even loaned us some to take home to read.

Uncle John's farmhouse had no indoor toilet, so when we visited him and his family, we had to use the outhouse for number one and number two. I entered it with dread because it also stank. I held my nose for as long as I could and then breathed in through my fingers. That made it more difficult to poop, prolonging my agony. Afterwards, I inspected the hole by opening the door to let in some light and fresh air. The different forms and colors of human poop amazed me—some hard, some gooey, some with yellow splotches, others almost black. What wondrous and varied creatures we must be!

A ONE-HOLE FACILITY WITH A LIMIT

Uncle John's outhouse only had one hole for sitting on and I wondered how the McKee family had managed when my father was a child in the 1920s. My grandparents had nine children and if you counted my grandfather's parents, who also lived in the tiny farmhouse, 13 people had to line up every morning. Maybe they all had to draw numbers out of a hat. It would have been real torture waiting outside and equally painful if you happened to be the one inside. I have always found it hard to go when others are waiting outside the door, telling you to hurry up. What a way to start the day!

The barnyard also stank—full of cows and pigs standing in their own poop. Kind of disgusting, really, like ostriches, only you could actually see these beasts apparently enjoying themselves. I liked the fields surrounding the barnyard better, especially after Uncle John had ploughed most of the animal dung into the soil.

During these visits to the farm, I learned a lot about manure and why the farms surrounding Elmira made our town stink so much, especially when the wind blew from the west and north. Dad told us the smell came from Old Order Mennonite farmers' fields, and like at Uncle John's, they didn't have indoor toilets—not even running water or electricity. These farmers traveled to and from town in various models of buggies drawn by one or two horses. For short visits, they would tie up their beasts to posts behind the stores, where they had to wait patiently, while dropping large piles of dung on the ground. In Western movies I also saw rows of horses waiting out front for cowboys to finish their drinks in saloons, but their horses weren't allowed to poop on the street. In comparison to Mennonite horses, those cowboys' horses were well-behaved.

Mennonites' clothes were also way different from cowboy gear. The Old Order men wore breaches held up with suspenders, blue shirts, and black coats and hats. The women were clothed in dark dresses, shawls, and hooded bonnets, much like those worn by women in storybooks about people who lived 100 years ago. Mennonite men normally appeared in town clean-shaven, but some older women had mustaches and faint beards. My dad said it came from inbreeding—generation upon generation of cousin marriages in their close-knit communities. Most adults wore old-fashioned wire spectacles because they didn't eat enough carrots, or so Mom told us. But I wondered if it was only a ploy to get us to eat everything on our plates, including her over-boiled vegetables. Mom always ate everything on her plate and became somewhat chubby, but never fat. I think Dad liked her that way.

Pigs provided another variety of smells in our town. Until the early 1950s, Elmira's town center featured a pig auction on the first Tuesday of every month—corrals full of the squealing beasts being offloaded and loaded onto trucks and herded back and forth in confusion, as men shouted out the prices they were willing to pay. Those Tuesdays, the whole shopping district smelled of fresh pig dung, adding to the town's standard cologne.

Next to the auction, stood a horse and buggy parking garage called the "Farmers' Shed." It provided shelter for horses from wind, rain, cold and snow, especially for longer-term visits to town. It also produced a daily pile of horse shit. But you couldn't say "shit," so

our parents told us to call them "horse buns." The Old
Order Mennonites were then, and remain today, an honest hard-working Christian tribe who dealt only in hard
currency—no credit, no checks. The town council and
merchants didn't mind hauling away the horse buns,
while keeping the cash.

Mennonites' horses also deposited a daily download
on the streets of Elmira. This abundant output provided
employment for old Ben, a civil servant with a broom,
a shovel, and a wheelbarrow. Old Ben lived in a shack
along the creek, next to the slaughterhouse on the north
side of town. He had weather-beaten skin, a bald head,
and wore ragged dirty overalls. He liked to sing while
he worked on the streets. He also whistled, winked, and
joked with teenage girls and some of the younger women

OLD BEN'S NEVER-ENDING JOB

who walked by. "Hi there, sweets! What's you doin' later? Wan'a ride in my wheelbarrow?" But he had no teeth, so few people could understand what he said. Despite this, they laughed when he laughed at his own jokes.

Some of the older boys would tease old Ben and try to get him worked up, "Old Ben screwed a hen and now chicks pass from his ass."

But old Ben would be the first to defend himself, raising his middle finger in the air and spewing forth a stream of foul words. I think those guys teased him just to increase their own vocabulary.

As I recall, Mennonite-owned horses only provided part of the reason for old Ben's gainful employment. In those days, horse-drawn wagons and carts delivered blocks of ice to those houses that hadn't upgraded from iceboxes to refrigerators. Horse-drawn carts also brought us groceries and milk. The milkman's horse and cart would meander through the streets, clip-clopping along, temporarily halting, then advancing in tandem with the milkman, allowing him to exit and enter on both sides, never missing a customer's veranda, where empties and cash payments lay waiting.

Periodically, the horses would deposit a fresh pile of horse buns, ready to be squished by passing cars. They looked like pancakes and remained there until old Ben got around to scraping them up and hauling them away in his wheelbarrow.

For some reason, I didn't mind the odor of sweating horses. One day, this brought me great luck. I was playing beside a line of tired horses, resting while tied up by the back door of Hendrick's Hardware. As I walked up the ramp leading to the door, I spotted a bright-blue,

Canadian, five-dollar bill on the ground below, behind a horse's hind hooves. I could see our young Queen Elizabeth's face peering out through a pile of horse buns, and so I jumped down like superman to rescue her. Who wouldn't? That was big money!

OUR QUEEN IN DIRTY DANGER

After running home, giving the bill a careful cleaning in the kitchen sink, and smoothing it out on the counter, I presented it to my mother, "See what I found?"

"Where'd you find it?"

"Behind Henrick's Hardware under a pile of horse buns."

"Well, it's good you washed it. Did you wash your hands with soap afterwards as well?"

"Yes, mommy."

"We had better report it to the lost and found."

"No, it's mine."

"You've been lucky, but it's not yours."

"Please...."

"Well, if you want to keep it, you have to share. Buy something the whole family can enjoy."

Her argument didn't make much sense to me, but I felt my shoulders slump as I gave up. I'd been beaten by my own honesty. My parents had recently bought a new record player, so Mom took me to the music store where she helped me buy some records, including a copy of *The Noisy Eater*, spoken and sung in the high and scratchy voice of Jerry Lewis.

I wanted this record to be pure comedy for my siblings and me to enjoy, but it ended in a preachy lesson, like Mom's on sharing my good luck. After listening to it over and over, I figured the producers had badgered Jerry Lewis into teaching us kids a moral, which went something like this: "If you slurp your soup, chew your food with your mouth open, or reach across the table for more food instead of politely asking for it to be passed to you, you'll be sent away from home with only a small suitcase containing your toothbrush, pajamas, jackknife, and your frog."

The record was really short, but I remember how Jerry, the noisy eater, wandered alone for days, having many adventures. Then, after staying with an old couple—the noisiest, most disgusting eaters in the whole world—he decided to go back home with better table manners, and his parents gave him a five-dollar bill as a reward, telling him that he could buy anything he wanted with it. In the story, Jerry didn't mention what he bought, but he certainly had more luck than I had, because he didn't have to share. At first, his banishment seemed like pure punishment to me— much worse than being whacked on the head with a tablespoon—which Dad often threatened but rarely carried out.

As I grew older, I often thought about Jerry Lewis— freely wandering down far-away roads with his suitcase, bathed in sunshine and inhaling pure air. He had a better chance of finding many more five-dollar bills than I'd ever have. Bit by bit, it dawned on me: for now, I'd just keep on the go to avoid the worst stinks, but I didn't have to stay in this town forever.

IRISH TWINS WITH KAREN, ME ON THE RIGHT

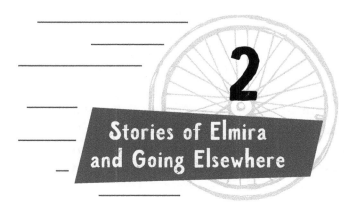

2

Stories of Elmira and Going Elsewhere

For the first few years, my brother Glen and I looked somewhat alike. I thought it was probably because of the identical clothes Mom bought us that some people called us "Irish twins." When I was old enough to be curious, while eating lunch one day, I asked Mom about the twin business. "How come they call Glen and me Irish twins? You told me I'm a year younger than he is and I have a larger nose, one bigger ear, and a gap between my front teeth."

Mom shot me a surprised look and said, "You're exactly a year less nine days younger. You're not twins. I just had you close together. Some people say that's like having twins. Anyway, not all twins look alike."

"You said that Dad's a twin, and he looks exactly like Uncle Gerald."

"Yes, they're identical twins."

"He said his family came from Scotland. So, are they identical Scottish twins?"

"No, they're Canadian."

To add to my confusion, I had been told our cousins David and Alec Neill were twins, and their mother, Aunt Doreen, was my father's older sister. She had married one of my mother's older brothers, Uncle Addison. [I later deduced that made my Neill cousins my double first cousins. My parents had given me my mother's maiden name, Neill, as my first name.]

I continued, "You said the Neills came from Ireland."

"Yes, that's right."

"So, are David and Alec Irish twins?"

Mom replied, "No, Neill. Neill is an Irish name but David and Alec aren't Irish twins. They're not identical twins either—they look different. But they were born on the same day, in fact the same day as your sister, Karen."

Karen, three and a half years older than me, was quite small, slim, and pretty, with fine dark hair. She didn't look much like David and Alec. My brain began to fog up with this new information from Mom. I started to formulate the words for asking about my sister's candidacy for being an Irish triplet when Mom abruptly said, "Now eat your sandwich."

At first, we lived in an apartment on Church Street, one of the only streets in town without any churches, unless you counted the Mennonite churches on the hill by the western border of Elmira. A Mennonite lady, Mrs. Brubacher, lived downstairs. My parents called her a "new Mennonite" but she didn't look that new to me. She wore heavy black shoes, a fine white hairnet, and long dark dresses decorated with various small flower patterns. On Mondays, when all women in town did their laundry, you could see those dresses on her wash line, so I knew she had at least five, counting the one she most likely had on at the time.

Anyway, Mom often told the story that when she brought me home from the hospital, Mrs. Brubacher took one look at me and declared, "I'm sorry Alma, but you won't raise him." When I came into this world, I was evidently all withered and wrinkled like a little old man. [Years later, I concluded my mother was breast-feeding my brother and that robbed me of a lot of nutrients while I was in her womb—a major problem one can encounter when entering the world as an Irish twin.]

In spite of Mrs. Brubacher's dire prediction, in a couple of months, rolling in baby fat, my parents took me to our church's baptismal font for the obligatory sprinkling. Elmira had 13 Christian churches competing for about 3,000 souls, so infant baptism couldn't be avoided, unless you were born into a Mennonite family. They waited until their children became teenagers before baptism and then, I heard, they got dunked—no light sprinkling for those Mennonite kids.

As soon as I could think through the matter, the Mennonite approach to baptism seemed completely reasonable to me. People should have the choice of getting baptized or not. What infant ever has the life experience to make such a decision? I came to observe that even the mild form of baptism, sprinkling water over babies' heads in front of the whole congregation, distressed them. They usually hollered and then all the adults would sadistically chuckle and look at each other with satisfied smirks. For a time, I wondered if this could be a test to determine if a child should live or die.

From an early age, I learned stories about the Mennonites who lived in and around Elmira. I listened to them carefully and sometimes I became confused because they switched back and forth between English and what Dad said was "Pennsylvania Dutch." As I grew older, I learned they were actually speaking Pennsylvania Deutsch, a Low-German dialect. [English speakers mistakenly call them and their language, "Pennsylvania Dutch." Their ancestors migrated from southern Germany and Switzerland to Pennsylvania. They are pacifists and because of the violence of the American Revolution and its aftermath, beginning around 1800, many of them immigrated to Ontario, then called "Upper Canada." Some joined later, coming directly from Europe. They liked the fact that their northern neighbors had fewer guns because the British Crown still managed law and order in Canada. Like most people at the time, Mennonites had many children and they also needed to find new and cheaper land for their sons, and farmer husbands for their daughters. Only farming would do. Other worldly occupations would have invited too many temptations and evils into their lives.]

Besides the two Mennonite churches on the hill, Elmira had a variety of other Christian churches because the townspeople came from many places they called the "old country," such as England, Scotland, Ireland, Germany, Poland, Holland, Russia, Ukraine, Norway, and Sweden. I don't recall any Italians or Greeks, but some people changed their surnames to sound like English names, so it was hard to tell.

A CLASH OF HEAVENLY LUTHERAN MUSIC

There were two large Lutheran churches, St. James' and St. Paul's, whose members didn't talk to each other much because they disagreed on the true meaning of different Bible verses, or so I was told. Both churches had tall steeples and towers to broadcast competing chimes from their bells, or music from their carillons, on Saturday at 5 p.m., warning everyone that the Sabbath was drawing near.

My family attended the United Church, a 1925 union of the Methodists, Congregationalists, and most Presbyterians in Canada. I recall a separate Presbyterian church whose congregation didn't like some of the methods of the Methodists; a small and plain Anglican chapel; and a stately Roman Catholic edifice—a forbidden place to us because, we were told, Catholics follow the Pope and worship statues of a tortured Jesus with blood dripping down his legs onto the bottom of the cross. They also worship his mother, Mary, a practice which some people said was "sacrilegious," although I wasn't clear on what that meant.

21

By contrast, our old Trinity United Church on Arthur Street had plain dark wood furnishings with only one simple cross and no statues at all—kind of a dull place. The pews didn't even have cushions, so people with sore bottoms—Dad called it "hemorrhoids"—had to avoid church, especially if the preacher's sermons were long. I recall you could predict the hymns and Bible stories by the time of year, and the sermons delivered by Reverend Metcalfe put me to sleep. On Christmas and Easter, he would call the children to the front to deliver a special message in a quieter voice. These Bible stories were mainly of the "gentle Jesus, meek and mild" variety. But one Sunday, I woke up when he read a more interesting story about Jesus:

> And when he had made a scourge of small cords, he drove them all out of the temple, and the sheep, and the oxen; and poured out the changers' money, and overthrew the tables; and said unto them that sold doves, "Take these things hence; make not my Father's house a house of merchandise."

Now this story could keep a kid awake. But Rev. Metcalfe didn't dwell on such tales, probably because we had too many bankers and businessmen in our congregation. Members of our church professed a more liberal form of Christianity in which you didn't have to declare you had sinned every Sunday, holding your hands up to heaven. Our congregation included many of the town intelligentsia, men such as chemists, engineers, and teachers—people who knew they were right about most things due to their superior educations.

One day, my cousin Alec pointed out a different kind of church—the Pentecostals. He called them "Holy Rollers." I went back to look inside through their church's window, but I couldn't see anyone rolling. So, the next time I saw Alec, I told him, "They don't roll on the floor. They wave their arms all around and speak some strange words. It sounded funny to me."

Alec replied, "Sure. They speak in tongues."

"Who do they speak to?"

"To God."

"Is that God's language?" I asked.

"Yes, I can teach it to you sometime."

"Do they baptize their babies?"

Alec replied, "For sure. They push people into a river—a real dunking."

"In our town creek? It's pretty dirty."

"God washes them clean if they speak in tongues."

My cousin knew so much more than I did, and the fact he could also speak God's language tripled my admiration for him. In spite of learning they didn't roll on the floor, I liked how they rocked back and forth because I rocked myself to sleep in bed most nights, a comforting sensation I can highly recommend, at least up to age ten. After that people might think you've got real problems.

We had other churches in Elmira—the Baptists, plus a few other reformed and fundamentalist Bible chapels. I can't recall any synagogues in our town, though a Jewish guy by the name of Conrad owned a scrap metal business—a great place for finding bargains. If he did go to a synagogue, it was probably in Kitchener-Waterloo.

At the Old Order Mennonite church on the west side of town, at least 100 horses and buggies would park on

MENNONITE HORSES PATIENTLY WAITING

Sunday morning, all lined up along a fence, pooping on the ground, while the people sat inside their little white church, praying and singing in Pennsylvania Deutsch. I wondered how they could tell their horses apart because so many of them looked alike to me—dark brown or black. Mennonites couldn't own light brown, white, or pinto beasts of burden—too showy. When the service ended, the men would retrieve their horses and buggies to pick up their wives and children at the front door, then prance up the gravel shoulder of Highway 86.

Grown-ups in town told stories of how the new Mennonites had to follow different color codes for their cars, depending on decisions made by their congregations—some painted completely black, even the chrome fenders and hubcaps. Some churches allowed chrome, while others permitted chrome and various colored vehicles—but nothing too flashy. Each congregation set its own rules and elected a deacon from its members to serve for about five years—a renewable term, so some became almost life-long preachers. The deacons also had to study the Bible, visit the sick and bereaved, and ensure all members held to the rules, usually decided by the whole group. Those who didn't would find themselves shunned by the rest.

On Sunday mornings, the roads in and around Elmira clogged up with horses and buggies, as well as flashy Fords, Chevys, and Plymouths, driven by mainstream Protestants and Catholics. The exhaust fumes from all these vehicles added to the standard toxins in the air.

People in Elmira liked to tell stories. Dad often repeated the story of how Elmira got its name: "One spring, over 100 years ago, when an English settler arrived with his wife Maira, their ox-cart became stuck in the mud and he swore, 'Ell, Maira, let's go 'ome!'"

Before television came, telling such stories was a main form of entertainment, more so than reading books, listening to radio, or going to the cinema. Most people in Elmira worked all week so they could take breaks at lunchtime to tell stories. They shopped, played sports, or fixed their houses and mowed their lawns on Saturday, stopping to trade stories when they saw an opportunity. They went to church on Sunday to listen to Bible stories and then repeated more of their own stories after the service ended. I must admit, I found most of these accounts rather dull and repetitive, except for tales about going elsewhere.

We didn't have to go very far to come up with great stories. On some Sundays after church and lunch, our parents would take us for drives in the countryside.

This may sound great, but I should first explain that the upholstery in our old Plymouth had a dusty smell. Also, its back doors swung open on hinges to the rear. Glen liked to play with mechanical things and one Sunday, while we traveled along a gravel road, he jerked the right back door handle, causing the door to open and catch the wind. I was seated in the middle of the back seat, Karen on the left, and our parents in front. Suddenly, Glen disappeared. I tried to alert Dad about his absence but he ignored me, so I thought maybe Glen had gone out to pee or something.

Then Karen shrieked, "Glen fell out!"

Dad braked quickly and the door slammed shut. He reversed the car as his first-born son came running up the road shouting, "Hey, wait for me!"

As it turned out, Glen had bounced off the gravel and landed on a grassy shoulder, so he only had a few scratches. As usual when distressed, Dad stroked the back of his head with his left hand and muttered, "What knuckleheads designed such a stupid car? Glen's head could have been smashed by the door!"

HEY, WAIT FOR ME!

26

He didn't say so, but probably he was also bemoaning the fact that he had been dumb enough to buy this model. He vowed, then and there, to trade in the car for a safer one as soon as he could save up enough money. In the meantime, forever the innovator, he installed his own brand of leather seat belts.

After Mom got her driver's license, we took some fabulous trips to Toronto, 80 miles (129 km) away. In late August, we usually went with Mom's sister Elsie and our cousins who lived in Streetsville. We'd all head off to Toronto for the Canadian National Exhibition—an enormous fair with many wondrous sights: a huge troop of red-coated Royal Canadian Mounted Police marching to music in ever-changing formations; a humongous pavilion with food samples; a 700-pound woman who would get up to wiggle ever so slightly to music, and then sweat all over; a seven-foot giant with a three-foot dwarf friend; a ferris wheel and a roller coaster so much higher and faster than those at Elmira's puny fall fair. They'd turn your stomach inside out. Such trips provided many fantastic stories to tell our friends back home.

The grossest story happened one year when we drove through downtown Toronto. Karen often suffered from car sickness, so Mom wisely brought along thick paper bags, just in case. That day, Karen had to puke and managed to deposit most of it in a bag. But it still smelled terribly and I complained. After a fruitless search for a trash bin, Mom and Aunt Elsie decided to stop and quickly drop the bag at curbside, then take off as fast as possible.

Unfortunately, a red light brought them to a halt and a man came dashing up beside the car, holding the bag and yelling, "Hey, ladies, you dropped your lunch!" He handed it back through the window and we all laughed. We continued to chuckle over this story no matter how many times it was repeated.

The great thing about my parents was that they took us on summer holidays to different places. They never wanted to own a cottage on a lake, which would have required upgrades and repairs, and an obligation to return to the same place every summer. They preferred variety.

One summer we took a trip up through Bruce Peninsula, which partly divides Georgian Bay from the rest of Lake Huron. Dad bought a small oval trailer for the trip. It held our clothes, food, and campfire cookery. Our parents slept inside, while we slept in a tent outside, forever guarding against mosquitoes and strange noises—most likely raccoons but possibly bears—which would be very exciting. We much preferred this arrangement; so, our parents allowed us to practice camping— raising the tent and sleeping in our backyard for a few nights before we left.

On such camping holidays, Dad made obligatory stops for possible sales of his farm equipment, or to check how his former farm customers were doing. During our trip up the peninsula that year, we camped at one of those farms. While Dad and Mom visited the couple, their kids took us into a cool dark cave where people had found human remains and ancient relics. It may have been a burial ground—a sacred place of the Ojibwe people. At least it made a good story.

Next, we traveled by ferry from Tobermory to Manitoulin Island on Lake Huron, the largest freshwater island in the world. We explored this forested land, dotted with small settlements, occasional gas stations, and stores selling bait and Indian crafts. We spent our allowances and earnings on wooden tomahawks or headdresses with colorful feathers. [On reflection, most of these crafts consisted of crass souvenirs—distortions of the arts and crafts of people who once occupied the whole island. Much later I learned this "First Nation" or "Indigenous People," as they came to be called in Canada instead of "Indians," could have told me many great stories about their battles with the invading Iroquois; their banishment to far-away lands; their return to resume worshiping the forest, its wildlife, and waters with plentiful fish—all provided for their sustenance by the Creator.]

FINE FEATHERED FRIENDS

Even when Dad rented cottages for the family at Honey Harbour on Georgian Bay, I don't think we stayed in the same place twice, and I liked it that way— better to see features of the lake and forest from different angles over time, to gain a complete picture. The eastern shore of the bay provided a summer playground for the people of southern Ontario, at least those who could afford it. Westerly winds passed over thousands of rocky islands covered with spruce and pine trees, cloaking our surroundings in slightly scented air. I would take deep restorative breaths as we hiked in the woods, played on the sandy beach, swam in cold water, fished from the dock or our motorboat, and watched hot ashes rise from our campfire on their way to join the stars twinkling between dark pine branches.

We also made some special trips to Niagara Falls, only a two-hour drive from Elmira, to see the flowers in spring and stare at the mesmerizing water tumbling in a horseshoe shape on the Canadian side, a much more majestic close-up view than from the American side.

On one occasion, Dad took us to visit Fort George, where the British Army fought the Americans in the War of 1812. I was too young to remember but I later learned in school the story of this place. It was where the famous Major-General Sir Isaac Brock was shot in the chest and died in the Battle of Queenston Heights. We learned how his valiant men rallied late in the day, with the help of native warriors and Canadian militia, repelling the American invaders and forcing their surrender or retreat. Our side took about 1,000 Americans prisoners that day—a major victory which helped to keep Canada separate from the U.S.

Some Sunday afternoons, we took trips to visit Uncle Leigh, Aunt Hazel, and our Neill cousins who lived in Port Robinson, Ontario, a village situated along the Welland Canal. I watched in awe as the bridge lifted and giant ships suddenly cruised through the town. They hauled cargo between Lake Erie and Lake Ontario. The very sight of these monsters cutting through Port Robinson signaled to me there was a big world out there to be explored, full of different stories.

However, my greatest childhood story of going elsewhere was when we went out West in the summer of 1957. Glen and I traveled with our parents on a Trans-Canada Air Lines Lockheed Super Constellation to Winnipeg, Manitoba, where we caught one of their North Stars to Calgary, Alberta. I shivered with excitement to the rumble of those huge propeller engines taking us 2,000 miles (3,219 km) into the unknown.

GOING OUT WEST, 1957

At the Calgary Stampede, we had our picture taken with a Blackfoot chief in full-feather regalia. We witnessed a parade through the city, the rodeo, chuckwagon races, and cowboys performing tricks with ropes. I remember Roy Rogers and Dale Evans prancing by on their horses and tipping their hats to us.

Dad, as usual, had business to attend to at the Stampede, selling his hay harvesters. While fooling around at his sales display, we heard the never-ending, next-door invitation from a barker to "Come and see Mokondo, the blood-sweating river horse from the River Nile." We couldn't resist, so we "came and saw!"

When we paid ten cents each to walk up the ramp and peer into the cage, we could only see a fat old wrinkled hippopotamus—no sweating blood at all. The poor beast seemed in great distress—all dried up because of its confinement. It should have been

WITH A BLACKFOOT CHIEF AT CALGARY STAMPEDE

DAD SELLING HIS HARVESTERS BESIDE MOKONDO

bathing in the rivers of Africa. But just the same, to my 11-year-old eyes, Mokondo appeared otherworldly, like the rest of "out West."

These are only some of the stories that compensated for my being born an "Irish twin" who barely survived an early death and had no choice about being baptized. I periodically escaped my hometown's factory stinks, clashing bells and carillons, buggies and cars, to see a larger and more exotic world out there, waiting to be explored. I was lucky my parents had enough money to help me become a "kid on the go!"

OUR NEW "FORTRESS" ON DUKE STREET

3

First Dreams of Africa

Going back to the early 1950s, Dad and Uncle Gerald's farm equipment manufacturing business, McKee Brothers Limited, was rapidly expanding and they built a new factory in 1952, which stood beside the chemical and fertilizer factories on the east side of town.

They also bought a large square yellow-brick house on Duke Street, only a few blocks away from their new factory. Uncle Gerald and Aunt Lillian lived upstairs

MCKEE BROTHERS' NEW FACTORY ON UNION STREET

while we lived downstairs, until our families grew too large. Then we took over the whole fortress—two finished floors, an attic, and a cellar all to ourselves—while Gerald bought another house.

A dank odor pervaded the cellar. Its white stone walls held shelves of sealed glass jars, filled with preserved fruit and pickled vegetables. In late summer, Mom made pickles from cucumbers, a process which filled the whole basement with a sour vinegary stench. I got used to this short-term pain for long-term gain. I liked pickles, especially the sweet ones, which would last until next fall's harvest.

Our parents told us to keep out of the coal bin, filled with lumps of the black stuff, which fed our hungry old furnace. When we played in it, the coal left black smudges on our clothes and bodies, evidence that we'd disobeyed. Later, Dad spoiled our fun by ordering the installation of a new oil-burning furnace with a foul-smelling tank.

Glen and I also played in the basement's sandbox, especially in winter, when it hid our carrots and potatoes—a cheap dehumidifier-refrigerator all in one. One day when I was about seven or eight years old, I played with an older neighbor girl in our cellar sandbox. Suddenly, she said, "I'll show you mine if you show me yours." I didn't know what she meant until she showed me hers. It seemed quite a natural thing to do but then she told me not to tell others about our peeking exchange. I don't think she knew any more about sex than I did, but it did make our carrots and potatoes a little more interesting at supper time.

When I played outside, I kept on the go. It seemed

to help block the town's odors from entering my nostrils. I can still remember the pleasant fragrance of fried hamburger at lunchtime, coming out of our kitchen window beside the gas cylinders in our backyard. That's when I slowed down and started to breathe deeply again.

From our fortress, we could easily reach the Canagagigue Creek, which served as a route out of Elmira. Everyone pronounced its name "Canakajig." When I was a kid, the adults all said the name came from the language of native Huron people who once populated the area. [Elmira residents preferred this story, although it may have been named by Mennonite settlers from southern Pennsylvania where there's a Conococheague Creek.]

The Canagagigue meanders in from the west along the north side of town and turns south along the eastern side, passing Naugatuck Chemicals. At the time, it also passed by the fertilizer factory and the town dump. In spring, the creek became a wide river with gigantic ice jams. Glen and I, with cousin David, would spend Saturdays exploring this transformation. David taught us to avoid getting "buggered," a word he used instead of "trapped."

When the snow and ice melted, various streams of the swollen creek joined and then separated. One branch would meander in a certain direction, seemingly lost, and then return to the home stream. If we weren't careful, we would explore for hours and then suddenly find ourselves "buggered" on an island with no visible way off, except by backtracking on our long and puzzling entrance route. Cold churning water often prohibited safe wading, but we would search for the shallowest fording place. We usually ended up with water pouring over the tops of our black and orange rubber boots, resulting in squishy and nearly frozen feet as we trudged home.

During the summers, we explored and fished in the creek downstream from the chemical factory, where DDT, 2,4-D, and 2,4,5-T were in full production. There, we came upon acidic festering pools and creepy things, such as frogs with two heads and fish with only one eye. We didn't try very hard to catch these fish, but if we happened to hook one, we'd throw it back in. They looked too spooky, almost ghost-like, and Mom never liked fish, anyway.

At suppertime, if we tried to tell Mom and Dad about these weird creatures of the Canagagigue, Dad would chuckle and Mom would say something like, "You're lucky to have meat and potatoes, unlike the children in Africa, so eat up all that's on your plate."

She obviously didn't know about the dangers of the creek we played in. Mom had a Grade 10 commercial education and could type, but as far as I could see, she only read *Reader's Digest* and the United Church

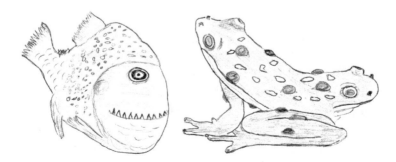

BEASTS OF THE CANAGAGIGUE

newsletters left on the top of the toilet tank. I can't recall many books in our house besides a set of Encyclopedia Britannica, purchased from a door-to-door salesman. It had pictures, so we could identify some of the creatures we found. These books, and a globe my parents bought us, were my window to a wider world. I would sit for a half-hour at a time, staring at the globe, twirling it in both directions and stopping it with my finger to see what continent and country I landed on.

Glen and I quickly learned not to talk too much about our latest wanderings and discoveries in order to protect our freedom against any declarations about places being "out of bounds." But we also knew our parents probably never would have had the means of surveillance and enforcement, other than locking us in our room—something they would never do.

Our big house served as my refuge from all the stinks and weird beasts I encountered in and around Elmira. It also featured a dumbwaiter, a small elevator box operated with ropes. It had been built into the wall for lifting things from the cellar to the kitchen and even to the second floor. We could fit inside, one at a time, and take turns pulling each other up and down between floors. Karen and Glen would sometimes help me into the apparatus on the second floor and then shout, "The rope's breaking. You're going to die!" But after a few times, I got used to their trick and didn't panic. I knew the box wouldn't plunge because Dad told me about pulleys and counterweights. It all sounded very mechanical, even scientific, and I trusted him more than my siblings when it came to knowledge about how things work.

Learning about gravity in our backyard was another matter. When I was around seven or eight years old, our pear tree became a place of exploration and it served as a ladder to the roof of our garage—a perfect height for parachuting, or so I thought. I'd seen a few World War II movies by then, and soldiers jumping out of airplanes was the best part. Parachutes can float you down into very different lands, where something both dangerous or magical might happen.

One day, I made a parachute from an old bed sheet, tying heavy strings at each of the corners and in between. I took a run from the top of the garage roof down the slope to its edge, leaping up and then plunging downwards. Glen, watching from above, later reported the sheet enveloped me as I hit the ground with a thud. He told me it looked "neat." Afterwards my back didn't feel so neat. It was a bit stiff for a few days, but the jump was totally worth it. I'd gained first-hand experience with gravity.

From our garage roof, I could also see a hill to the east beyond the chemical and fertilizer factories. On the hill stood large wooden shapes which, to me, looked like elephants and rhinos, and maybe one giraffe. From this vantage point, I had a clear view of what I called "Africa." I never ventured to the top of the hill to see what was actually there. The chemical and fertilizer factories, as well as the polluted creek, stood in the way. The figures on the hill changed color throughout the day and in different weather—black silhouettes against the sunrise, brown shapes among tall green grass waving in the wind, faint outlines appearing and disappearing in rain and mist, and glowing gold reflections as the sun began to set. To me, this was a sacred place of dreams and a destination I might have the good fortune to reach someday.

One summer, the three Steed girls put their stamp of approval on my identification of these distant figures. They lived in Angola, a country in Africa where their father was a United Church missionary. Mrs. Steed and Mom had worked together in the kitchen of the Ontario Agricultural College in Guelph before they both got married, and the two couples remained good friends.

Karen, Glen, and I played "Africa" with the Steed girls during their visit. We spent many hours on our

PLAYING AFRICA WITH THE STEED GIRLS

41

front lawn in African huts we made from sticks and blankets, wearing towels wrapped around our heads and bottoms. We sang an Angolan hymn for which I never learned the translation: *"Paandookoosookoo datay, Paandookoosookoo datay, Pa-a-a-andoo, Pa-a-a-andoo, Paandookoosookoo datay."* To me, the Steed girls had the luckiest of childhoods—to be living in Africa. They only had to come back to Canada for a year every seven years.

The Steed girls' visit provided much entertainment. Sometime after they left, Glen and I had to amuse ourselves by resorting to our experiments in gravitational pull. The steep stairs between the first and second floors of our large house provided the apparatus. We slid like firemen down the banister. One day, Glen grabbed my legs and dragged me all the way down the uncarpeted steps—bump, bump, bump. The next day, a bump also appeared on my abdomen. Mom took me to the doctor's office, where he declared I had a hernia.

A week later, I found myself in Kitchener-Waterloo Hospital. The doctor placed a cup-like thing of ether over my nose and mouth and asked me to count backwards from ten. I followed his orders, "Ten, nine, eight, seven, six, five..." as layers of soft blankets descended on me. Then no time later, I woke up with a beautiful woman in white beside me. She had smooth brown skin and smiled at me warmly, showing her sparkling white teeth and inviting red lips. She smelled like spring flowers. An angel? Was I in heaven?

Mom and Dad must have been with me, but I can only remember this lady. I had seen Reverend Steed's photos so I knew she came from Africa. I stayed in the hospital for almost a week to recover from the operation, a normal thing to do in those days, but I didn't mind. Every day I could talk and laugh with her, breathe in her perfume, and gawk at her large bosom. When they finally released me from the hospital, I didn't talk about her. She became my special private memory, further evidence of the existence of a far-away, purer world.

After I recovered, I got back to serious exploration with Glen and our friends. We climbed a tall willow tree beside a nearby drainage ditch to gain new perspectives and new possibilities. We discovered a use for the small dry roots around the base of the willow. They had holes running right through them. Dug up, cut to size, and lit up, our "cigaroots" had a bitter taste and made us cough, but at least it was something to do with the long wooden matches we "borrowed" from our kitchen. Besides, I liked the smell of burning sulfur.

One autumn afternoon, we found something else to do with matches. East of the willow stood the shirt and overall factory, and next to it lay a field of wild grass and tall goldenrod. By late September, those weeds would

SOURCE OF OUR FIREPOWER

turn brown and brittle. I'd seen in a Western movie how, in the fall, homesteaders protected their houses and barns by starting a controlled fire on the dry grass around them. That day, one of our friends and I decided to follow their example. (In truth, I've forgotten which friend it was so let me say Norman—Glen denies any involvement to this day.) We had barely started a small fire in the far corner of the field when, suddenly, flames erupted all around us. We tried to stamp them out, but they raged toward the factory like angry waving demons. Realizing the hopelessness of our situation, we made a run for it, sprinting down Union Street, passing the furniture factory, and around the block.

As we approached my house on Duke Street, we heard the wail of the town's fire siren. We headed past Mom in the kitchen and up to the safety of the attic, still a hot and stuffy place that time of year. I pulled open the east window to breathe properly. The pleasant smell of burning grass hit my nostrils, as the town's volunteer firemen arrived with their long bright-red truck. They pulled out their hoses and extinguished the advancing flames, just in time.

My relief, due to their fast and gallant action, mixed with fear of being found out. Norman and I vowed to keep our mouths shut and our heads down, hoping no one could identify us. From the attic window, I looked once more over the top of the chemical factory toward "Africa."

It was then that I began to seriously weigh my different options on going elsewhere.

A VIEW OF THE FIRE FROM A SAFE DISTANCE

MY FOUR-POUND PICKEREL FROM LAKE NIPPISSING

4

Going Fishing with Surplus Sons

Going fishing provided another form of diversion from the various confinements and odors of my hometown. It's not that dead fish don't stink when you lay them in the sun on a river bank too long, something I learned soon enough.

On firefly-lit evenings, we would use flashlights to spot long fat dew worms, which some people call "night crawlers," emerging from holes on damp park lawns, then grab them like hungry robins. If it hadn't rained earlier that day, we would water our own lawn in the late afternoon and wait for the worms to surface after dark. We had to be quick to prevent these dew worms from darting back into their holes. If they got halfway in, we'd try to tug them out, ripping some in half. Half worms didn't count in the competition over who could gather the most. We usually caught more dew worms than we could use, and it was hard to keep them alive on warm spring days while fishing. Besides, they began to stink too.

When we were around nine or ten, Glen and I would disappear on our bicycles with friends for the whole day, traveling up to nine miles (14.5 km) into the countryside to the Conestoga River at the Village of Glen Allan. In spring, when riding along on my bicycle, I'd push one nostril closed at a time to shoot out snot, propelling all the corruption onto the gravel road. On the one hand, Dad couldn't stand such behavior or spitting, so I never did it near him. On the other hand, he only had one form of "art"—variations of people dripping snot from their large noses into bowls, which he would draw for us, visiting cousins, and friends, and then laugh and laugh at his own weird sketches.

MY MEMORY OF DAD'S SNOT DRAWINGS

We hiked along the banks of the Conestoga, where the air would invigorate me—a complete cleanout—as I listened to the shrill call of red-winged blackbirds nesting on the river flats. Sometimes, we would sit by a bridge for hours with our fishing poles, patiently waiting for bites, and then yank them in. At first, we only had simple bamboo poles and whatever hooks, lines, sinkers, and bobbers we could afford to purchase at either Hendrick's or Weichel's hardware. Glen and I saved up our allowances and earnings for Johnson casting reels with tri-colored lines, which looked pretty neat but really didn't increase our catch of small chub, bass, sunfish, catfish, and—only occasionally—speckled trout. It required a lot of work to clean these bony fish, and we had to do that ourselves. Mom would dutifully fry them up for us, except for the catfish, which she threw away. She said catfish flesh tasted like a muddy river bottom and was too mushy to eat.

Luckily, our favorite places for fishing were upstream from Elmira's industrial runoff. The Conestoga River and Elmira's own polluted Canagagigue Creek, flowed into the larger Grand River. That river, in turn, picked up more pollutants from cities such as Kitchener, as well as chemical fertilizer runoff from farms, and then emptied into Lake Erie, which was quickly becoming a chemical soup in which only invasive species, such as smelts from the Atlantic, could prosper.

Fishing became a more serious business when we went with our dad, his brothers, friends, and employees. In April, when they got word the smelts were running in

Lake Erie, Glen and I would join them for an evening. We'd arrive on the shores of the lake in late afternoon and gather enough wood to build a giant bonfire. At dusk, the men would set the wood on fire to attract smelts. Thousands of these tiny creatures would swim frantically toward the bright light on shore. Men with rubber waders, which came right up to the top of their chests, would walk out in the water about 200 feet (61 meters) and then return, dragging fine-mesh nets between them, slowly moving toward the fire. If we were lucky, they'd capture school after school of these helpless creatures.

My brother and I had many duties—scooping smelts out of the nets into buckets, keeping the fire fueled, watching the men with their nets in the dark water, gazing upwards to catch a glimpse of shooting stars, learning new puns on "smelts" and stinky "smells," and listening to stories of "surplus sons"—those of my father and all but one brother who had left the farm on which they were born, seeking their futures elsewhere.

My father and his hardworking brothers had a very different childhood. Because of the death of their father in a farm accident in 1933, they missed a lot of fun like we had. I heard how Dad and his brother Gerald had to quit school after completing Grade 8, to take over from their older brother Jim, who decided the time had come to declare himself "surplus." Jim wanted more gainful and exciting employment, and who could blame him?

Because my grandparents, Alex and Blanche McKee, had produced seven sons and two daughters, as soon as they could, Dad and Uncle Gerald gladly declared themselves surplus too. They left their four younger brothers in charge and escaped the dangerous drudgery of farm work to carry out what became their lifelong mission of designing and manufacturing safer and more efficient farm equipment that could prevent accidents, like their father's tragic death.

The stories grew in length and depth on our annual fishing trips to Lake Nippissing, a destination which lies 290 miles (467 km) north of Elmira, positioned around the same latitude as Sault Ste. Marie or Duluth, Minnesota, although we still considered the trip "going up North." The word "Nippissing" means "little water" in Ojibwe, a comparison with the Great Lakes. Nippissing is a medium-size lake, from which the French River flows into Georgian Bay on Lake Huron. It is only 15 to 20 feet (4.5 to 6 meters) deep, with many small islands providing shallows—ideal for catching northern pike; smallmouth bass; yellow perch; muskellunge, which we called "muskie"; and native walleye, which we called "pickerel."

Our fishing gang would descend on Lake Nippissing during the weekend closest to Queen Victoria's birthday, May 24, which was then and remains a holiday in English Canada, even though she died in 1901. By then, Dad had upgraded Glen and me to new Johnson Spin-Cast reels with monofilament lines—the very latest thing. We all stayed at Sarah's fishing camp on the South River, which flows into the lake's southern-most point. Sarah, who came from southern Ohio, cooked our bacon and eggs in the morning with a cigarette perpetually dangling from her lips. She told stories with a croaky southern twang, often interrupted by a relentless smoker's cough.

Sarah made eggs to order but with bits of saliva flying from her mouth, and cigarette ashes floating gently downwards on her frying pan—obligatory ingredients I could see against the sunlight beaming through the east windows. She'd ramble on, "I been comin' up North to these parts for over 20 years. It's God's country, *hack, hack.* Y'all don't know how lucky you are. Down in O-haa-o, there's just too many factories nowadays. If I had my druthers, I'd stay put up here year-round, but got too much family down South, *hack, hack....*"

Uncle Gerald would intervene from time to time, saying something comical like, "Sarah, that's enough spice on my eggs. Can you turn mine over and fry them on the other side?" The men would chuckle but politely eat what she served them anyway—no offense and no waste.

Observing this morning ritual, I learned to skip the eggs and make bacon and jam sandwiches, which I highly recommend, even today. The toaster was self-service and the bacon simmered in a pan on the far side of Sarah's old wood stove, out of range of most of her personal condiment projections.

Dad and Uncle Gerald came of age in the height of the depression when they learned frugality. They made their own fishing boats out of plywood, modest 15-foot crafts powered by 25- or 30-horsepower outboards. Dad liked to think up new designs. He even made his own boat trailer with layered steel springs running from the front to behind the wheels, over 10 feet (three meters) long. These springs had to be released for lowering the trailer at shoreline, both to unload and load the boat. When Glen and I grew strong and heavy enough, we had to hold down the springs at the front, so someone could pull out the retainer pins. When we let go of both springs, they'd swing up and back with such force that we had to jump clear to avoid being catapulted into the water. Dad often talked about getting a patent for his design, but I doubted it could pass a consumer safety test—maybe for a rocket launcher!

Uncle Jim wasn't impressed with his younger brothers' inventions and craftsmanship. After leaving the home farm, he became a miner and then a bush pilot in Northern Ontario. Jim had a penchant for building contraptions and one year he brought his pontoon boat to Lake Nippissing. Powered by a noisy and smelly airplane engine with a huge propeller, it could outrun all the other boats on the lake.

He also brought along his mother, Grandma Blanche McKee, then in her mid-60s. She had always been a resourceful person with courage. She had started teaching school at age 16. After her husband's death, she kept the farm while she and her oldest daughter, Doreen, raised all the younger children. Then, when Uncle John took over the farm in the mid-1940s, she went back to teaching. She never remarried. As she got older, Grandma McKee moved around between the houses of her children, helping to raise her many grandchildren.

Grandma loved to fish. I can still picture her mounted on top of Uncle Jim's pontoon rig, seated on a flimsy lawn chair, knitting in hand, while they skimmed over the tops of waves on the lake, beating all the other boats to the agreed-upon fishing spot for the day. Then she would pull

FISHING ON LAKE NIPPISSING

out her rod, bait it with minnows or worms, and fish like all the men.

We'd congregate our boats in one spot so we could pass competitive comments and jokes back and forth, including too many puns on "pissing in Lake Nippissing," something those guys drinking beer would have to do more frequently, though always turned away from Grandma.

Our father, a cautious teetotaler, warned us, "Boating and drinking don't mix. Many drunken fishermen drown every year while peeing over the edge of their boats." To Dad, fishing was a serious hobby and he'd bring along a jar to pee into, before blessing the lake with our contributions.

Don Coleman, a heavyset salesman working for McKee brother, liked to drink beer and exaggerate past fishing exploits: "Remember opening day of 1952? Bet you we could've filled up our boats with pickerel

TONY YATES, UNCLE GERALD,
AND DON COLEMAM ON A LUCKY DAY

if it wasn't for the limit. I brought in the biggest, a 15-pounder. Never seen anything like it. Struggled with it for at least an hour."

Then, another salesman by the name of Tony Yates, chimed in, "No way, Coleman. You make it sound like you're the 'Second Coming'—Christ on Lake Galilee. As I recall, you were snagged on an old rubber tire."

Tony, originally from England, would often enter the fray, putting down fishy stories with the saying, "It is evident that you are inebriated by the exuberance of your own verbosity." Then everyone would laugh, in spite of the fact we'd heard his joke before. It all had to do with timing, and Tony was a master at that.

One day, while so caught up in this bantering, we didn't notice threatening storm clouds approaching. The wind and rain thrashed us as we beat our way toward the nearest shore. I shivered, seeing the concern on Dad's face as he navigated our little boat through the swells. But Uncle Jim fired up his propeller-driven craft and flew over the top of the waves with Grandma facing backwards, only sheltered by her raincoat.

We chased Jim's rig as fast as we could safely do so, finally reaching a cove that gave us some protection, while we waited out the storm. Then we bailed out our boats and got down to some serious pickerel fishing and more storytelling. Pickerel are more inclined to bite after a good rain. Also, the boat smelled better, temporarily, when washed clean of outboard gas and the stink of dying or dead fish and bait.

Many an evening sitting by our campfire, I got to hear old and new stories by or about surplus McKee sons who had left the home farm and gone out West. In 1944, Uncle Bud traveled west for harvest season on the prairies to earn some cash. But he missed Ontario and a certain young lady by the name of Margaret, whose father had a place near the McKee farm. So, he returned to marry and make a living by building silos. He did handstands on top of these 50-foot structures. Probably he was influenced by the old story of his grandfather John

FISHING GANG AT SARAH'S CAMP

doing the same when he built the first silo on the McKee farm. Later, Uncle Bud sold McKee Brothers farm equipment in Cookstown for a while, then started his own businesses. He became an excellent auctioneer chanter, a good husband, and the father of seven children.

Uncle Archie also headed out West to Saskatchewan in the fall of 1944. Right after he stepped off the train, as the story goes, a drunken Frenchman took a swing at him and knocked him out. Apparently, this guy didn't like the looks of Archie, who was blind in one eye due to an accident at birth, making him appear to squint. One version I heard was that he mistakenly thought Archie was winking at him. Fortunately, he didn't hit Archie in the good eye. After recovering, Archie made some money helping with the wheat harvest on nearby farms. Then he headed up to the mines in the Yukon, where he worked as a cook in a hotel and avoided guys who might deliver additional punches.

After a couple years, Archie returned to Ontario to sell McKee farm equipment, married Eva from the Ottawa Valley, and raised a family. Eventually he became a super real estate salesman in Elmira, an occupation that suited him because everyone said Archie had a way with people, including the womenfolk. He knew how to tell just the right entertaining story to make people warm to him, and then sell a house for a good price.

In another story, Uncle David—the youngest in the family, who actually got a high school education—stowed away on a train to the west coast and found a job working in the Vancouver stockyards for a while. He also came back East to marry an Elmira girl by the name of Shirley, and raise a big family. He moved to Quebec and became the McKee Brothers dealer in that province. But then he got into a squabble with Dad and Uncle Gerald over money—a story we never talked much about. When his relationship with the company ended, Uncle David sold cars for a while and then pulled out and spruced up some of his old high school drafting blueprints, which he used to talk his way into a job at a large papermill. He knew how to ask the right questions and quickly learned the technicalities. Eventually, he headed the whole department of graduate engineers.

My dad, Uncle Gerald, and Uncle John, who took over the family farm, never went out West in their youth. They approached life more cautiously, especially compared to their older brother, Jim. He was the most adventuresome and eventually moved his family to Red Deer, Alberta, where he started his own farm equipment business. He became a dealer for McKee Brothers products, but later he and his son Wayne manufactured and sold their own products, including manure spreaders. His brothers joked with him about his success in this line of business, for they said he was always good at "spreading bullshit."

Uncle Jim kept his pilot's license and owned a small airplane. Once every couple of years, he would fly his plane from Alberta back East to Ontario, Aunt Annie beside him, incessantly commenting on the scenery and just about everything else, as she was prone to do. Jim would take us for flights over Elmira, using a nearby cornfield as an airstrip, after getting permission from the Mennonite farmer who owned the land. Such flights excited me so much because of their new and distant perspectives. I could see all the routes we had taken out of town and plan new ones.

One time, when Jim took Glen up for a ride, they hit a downdraft while landing. The tail of the plane caught a loose wire attached to a fence pole, causing an abrupt crash into a clump of corn stocks beside the cleared strip. They provided a cushion, preventing injuries, so Jim patched up his plane with wire and tape and took off again. He must have burned up a ton of fuel that day to please us, but never cared about the cost.

Uncle Jim was a man of action and loved to joke. I remember his often-repeated warnings when he came to dinner at our place, "Pepper kills mountain goats." I never knew what he meant by this assertion, why people would feed pepper to mountain goats, nor what harm either pepper or mountain goats could do to me. But he possessed authority on the matter because he lived near the Rocky Mountains.

Once at Sarah's fishing camp on Lake Nippissing, Uncle Jim told us an exciting war story, which I remember well. It received my "surplus sons' prize," for elegance, detail, and delivery: "The Second World War broke out while I was a bush pilot up North near Sudbury. I wanted to enlist as a fighter pilot but then saw the number of planes shot down by the Germans—would've been suicide. I knew enough about fixin' engines, so they assigned me to the engineers' corps—better than gettin' shot at all the time. Our corps had to keep the trains going, takin' in fresh soldiers and supplies and bringin' back the wounded and the dead. I traveled right through Europe, a dozen countries—even made it to North Africa and as far as Iraq. The Nazis tried to bomb us many times, but we outfoxed them buggers.

"One day, I was checking out a train engine in Italy, traveling by motorcycle. Suddenly, I found myself trapped on all sides by German soldiers. I saw this hill beside a farmer's stone wall and took a run at it, flyin' up and over their heads. I could see them lookin' up at me, stunned at first—couldn't believe their eyes. Then bullets started whizzing around me. But I was really flying—too fast for them to draw a good bead on me. Came down on the road and got the hell out of there."

In the 1960s, when I saw Steve McQueen make a similar motorcycle jump to avoid capture by German soldiers in the movie, *The Great Escape*, it was, quite frankly, a letdown compared to the trajectory Jim reported to us a decade earlier.

However, the best fishing trip story I have to tell from those days is one of my own. One year, right before the trip to Lake Nippissing, I came down with German measles. I had a fever and small ugly red spots broke out all over my body. I cried so hard my face felt hot and I became extremely angry with the Germans. I truly understood why Uncle Jim had gone to war against them. Dad allowed Glen to go off fishing with our uncles and his friends, while he stayed home with me.

When I reflected on this many years later, I remembered how much Dad loved fishing and what a remarkable sacrifice he had made that year. I came to understand that, although his third child and second son, to my father I was not surplus at all.

5

On Guns, Religion, and Rituals

Guns became another route to a more exciting world for me. I had little interest in toy trains or inventors' kits from *Popular Science Magazine*—Glen's department. Unlike the Mennonites, my father and most of his brothers liked to hunt. As long as I can remember, he kept rifles and shotguns in a locked case at home.

Once when I was only three, I woke up in the middle of the night, put on my cowboy hat and holster with toy pistol—birthday presents—and entered my parents' bedroom. Mom woke up and asked, "Neill, what on earth are you doing up at this time?"

I replied, "I'm a nightrider."

My parents laughed in spite of the sleep disturbance. Mom sent the story to Art Linkletter's famous radio program, *Kids Say the Darndest Things* and Art read it on air. [Few people in Canada knew or mentioned the fact that the term "nightrider" referred to the Klu Klux Klan, an organization that fortunately had a relatively brief history in our country.]

I often listened to radio programs such as *The Lone Ranger*, and I could visualize all the action because I'd been living around Mennonites' horses from early childhood. I easily made the connection to the Old West. At the beginning of summer, I would spend hours with my neighborhood friend Norman, playing cowboys and Indians, an innocent activity to us. [Actually, this kids' game, played throughout Canada and the U.S. at the time, has its origins in the genocide of the majority of indigenous people during the previous centuries. I knew little of the full story, for no one talked about it.]

Playing cowboys and Indians was an antidote for all the time I had to spend in school. Kids had to be five

COWBOYS AND INDIANS

MY KINDERGARTEN CLASS
WITH ME BESIDE THE TEACHER (NOT MY CHOICE!)

years old in September to start half-day kindergarten and I had been born in November, so when I began I was almost six. My first two years at Riverside School remain a blur to me. I can only remember peeing my pants due to anxiety of some sort. Maybe it was being compared to others, especially girls, in the tasks Mrs. Evans put us through, which consisted of a lot of cutting with small dull scissors, pasting, coloring, singing the same old songs over and over, and chanting the sounds of letters and numbers written on the blackboard. We also had to copy them into our brown notebooks, using yellow pencils, trying not to make a mess to avoid being ordered to erase and start over.

Unfortunately, every summer Mom cut short my cowboy escapades by sending me and my siblings to vacation Bible school, an exceedingly mind-numbing tradition—more cutting, coloring, and singing, much like kindergarten. I liked some of the action stories, such as David killing Goliath with a slingshot, Noah putting pairs of animals on his ark while leaving all those awful people to drown, and God's son Jesus being nailed to a cross and left to bleed to death. I even learned that God had once been a baby-killer. He sent an angel of death to slaughter all Egyptian first-born boys because their king was just plain stubborn and wouldn't free the Israelites.

At any rate, if they really wanted to teach us about violence and mayhem, I thought these stories could have been much improved with guns. Fortunately, Bible school ended at noon, so I had the rest of the day to play out my weaponized fantasies.

From the late 1940s, for only 10 cents, my siblings and I would go to Saturday afternoon matinees at our town's Reo Cinema to see Hopalong Cassidy or Zorro, and other great Western heroes in action. Once, when I was very young, my cowboy daydreams morphed into real dreams, as Karen and Glen forgot about me when the show ended. An usher found me about the same time they returned to the rescue, interrupting a great dream of me and Zorro chasing a gang of thieves to the edge of a steep cliff.

When my parents bought a television for Queen Elizabeth's coronation in 1953, I began to disappear into that box for hours on Saturday mornings, standing side-by-side with the Lone Ranger and Tonto, riding along with Roy Rogers and Dale Evans, and backing up Wyatt Earp in Dodge City, as he gunned down outlaws. Norman and I would practice all the new tricks we saw with our cap guns. One of us would toss a nickel up in the air, while the other would draw and flip his pistols, catch them, and fire before the coin hit the ground.

Mom's mother, Grandma Effie Jane Neill, would provide a link, in my mind, to one of the most famous gangs in Western history. Grandma Neill moved to our place a few years after Grandpa, the Reverend John Addison Neill, passed away. She had been staying with Mom's older sister Elsie and family, but after we took over all of the big house on Duke Street, we had more room. Grandma Neill had limited mobility because she had broken a leg in a fall, and it never healed properly. She had long gray hair, which she bundled up into a white net. She wore long black dresses or ones with small flower patterns, like the Mennonite ladies.

Grandma Neill told us she was born in Wisconsin in 1876. She didn't mention it was around the time Jesse James and his gang were robbing banks and trains.

GRANDMA NEILL ON HER 80TH BIRTHDAY

She'd never talk about such things. But I figured out when Grandma was six, back in 1882, one of Jesse's own gang members shot him to death to collect the reward on his head.

One time, just to get her reaction, I asked, "Grandma, did you ever see Jesse James and his gang?" She gave me a disapproving scowl, a silent stare. I knew by then she didn't like guns. [She never talked about it, but years later I learned her father had been wounded in the Civil War, and it affected him for the rest of his life.]

In spite of her restrictions on talking about guns and outlaws, Grandma remained a very tolerant and non-judgmental person, and thankfully my parents didn't ban me from using cap guns or watching cowboy shows on television. That would have ruined my life.

Mom and Grandma made sure "The Golden Rule" governed all our activities: "Do unto others as you would have them do unto you." Sunday school, vacation Bible school, and their own brand of religious lessons emphasized this regulation—so easy to remember but hard to follow. For instance, once Glen hit me on the head with a hammer. Stunned at his inability to follow the Golden Rule, I planned my revenge. I had to wait until I'd gained the strength and weight necessary to wrestle him so I could "do unto him what he did to me."

A neighbor kid named Cale also provided a great challenge concerning adherence to the Golden Rule. He lived around the corner, but our backyards met through our gardens. He was over twice my size and had Down's syndrome, though back then people called him a "mongoloid." [I didn't know at the time that it's a racial slur against Asiatic people, the Mongols, once led by the famous Genghis Khan who ravaged and pillaged, conquering most of Eurasia.] Cale didn't ravage us or pillage our backyard, but I must say he had similar tendencies.

In spite of—or maybe because of—Cale's challenges, Mom encouraged us to play with him. He liked to come through our garden into our yard and take over the green swings. Dad made them for us, not for a child of Cale's weight and size. He would occupy the whole space, swinging and humming for hours, if we let him.

Mom warned us, "Don't tease him. He could trample you with his big boots." This caused nightmares of me being stomped to death, but I never told Mom.

Cale obviously had trouble understanding the Golden Rule. So, we learned to tie the garden gate shut or wind the swing chains together. If he got through those barriers, we'd give him a little time on the swings and then try to free them by teasing him, "Cale the whale ate a snail!" Then he would chase us, but with his big clumsy killer boots he couldn't climb worth a hoot. The pear tree in our backyard provided us a perfect escape route.

One day, right after a heavy spring rain, as Cale plodded through our very wet garden with his eyes on our swings, I got so fed up that I shot him with my cap pistols. He also liked playing cowboys and Indians, so he fell down dead on the spot, covering his newly-cleaned clothes in mud. Cale's mother saw it all from their backyard and I lost my cap pistols for two weeks. But it was worth the penalty to see him fall like that. By the expression on his face, I think Cale loved it too.

For real weapons, we learned to make slingshots, using whittled hardwood branches and cutting strips out of discarded rubber tubing from the dump. But these missiles had limited range and accuracy. We quickly graduated to bows and arrows, making the bows from the best springy branches we could find, mounting tough strings and rubbing them with paraffin wax. We used dried goldenrod shanks for arrows.

Around that time, Dad brought a little dog home from a business trip to Uncle Bud's place—a small black and brown Manchester Terrier. I named her "Peggy" and I also gave her a longer name, "Peggy-Peggra-Peg, Elizabeth-Lizzy-Liz, Gala-Poochie-Pup, McGee-McFee-McKee," or just "Peg" for short. I learned to call her using her full name.

For some reason, the little dog gravitated to me, and everyone in the family said she was "Neill's dog." I had watched the feats of Rin Tin Tin on TV, a German Shepherd that helped a boy named Rusty, who had been orphaned in an Indian raid. I imagined Peggy in the same role and she followed me on my hunting trips.

One Christmas, our parents gave Glen and me a real wooden bow and arrow set, which they told us to share. It even had arrows with feathers. We set up target practice in the backyard using cardboard boxes, and became pretty good archers. When Mom and Dad weren't looking, I tried to hit birds and squirrels, but failed in my aim. I didn't like the idea of sharing the bow and arrow, so I saved my money and bought a longer fiberglass bow—very powerful. I took it on treks with Peggy, hunting rabbits along the creek, but I always came home empty-handed.

PEGGY, MY FIERCE HUNTING COMPANION

We had more luck with rabbit traps. Glen and I made them, following a design he had found in a boys' magazine. We set them up in wintertime in the scrub bush along the drainage ditch which ran out of the town center. We built them to be do-no-harm structures, basically plywood boxes with lids that would fall shut when a rabbit tried to eat a carrot, as I saw in cartoons. We always released our prey because we didn't really want to kill them. Only once did our do-no-harm policy backfire when a rabbit escaped custody inside Dad's warehouse, where his employees made hay wagons. Our prisoner somehow got out and frantically leapt around the concrete floor, looking for an exit. Finally, in desperation, it took a dive into an open pail of paint thinner—a very quick, if not completely painless death. We both felt sorry for what we had done to Bugs Bunny's cousin, but we carried on with our catch and release activities, thereafter making sure we freed them outdoors.

Glen and I had to wait until we reached the age of 10 or 11 before we were allowed to have BB guns— air-powered weapons that could actually do a lot of damage if you shot someone in the face. Dad taught us the basics of gun safety and we set up real targets in our backyard, shooting toward our garden...as long as Cale wasn't in sight.

On one hot summer's night, our parents allowed my siblings and me to sleep on our front balcony. We talked and talked. We couldn't fall asleep because of a street lamp, which shone in our eyes. On a dare from Karen, I aimed my BB gun and fired. The bulb exploded and we all broke into laughter, which quickly subsided when I realized I might be in deep trouble. I slept fitfully that night, waiting for the dawn of judgment. In the morning, we vowed to say nothing. About a week later, I noticed the lightbulb had been replaced—another lucky escape!

When we were old enough, our firepower increased. Dad bought Glen and me Cooey .22 caliber rifles. With these firearms, we could easily hit those dirty rats in the town dump. The garbage trucks deposited plenty of waste food for the rodents, fattening them up into beautiful targets. In addition, the dump provided a treasure trove of materials for us to find between our acts of murder—old batteries, rubber tires, carriage wheels, boards, partially used pails of paint, bottles of acidic stuff, junked appliances, and all kinds of discarded leather, rubber tires, and plastic sheets—pretty much everything a kid needed.

With our single-shot .22 rifles, we had only one chance to hit our targets, forcing us to become even better marksmen. Sometimes in winter, Dad would take us to a bush outside of town where we could track rabbits through fresh snow. I liked learning to tell rabbit tracks from those of other animals, but I never liked the idea of actually killing harmless creatures, especially if I could see their eyes.

When I grew big enough to withstand the kick, I got to use Dad's old, double-barrel, 12-gauge shotgun, after he bought himself a brand-new pump action model. I joined his duck hunting party for a couple of autumns, traveling to the fields near Luther Marsh. This ritual involved putting out decoys in corn stubble and hiding behind blinds along fences, waiting for the ducks to fly in. Then we would blast our shotguns in unison and watch them fall from the sky. You couldn't see their eyes. I liked the smell of burnt gunpowder mixed with autumn leaves, but like Mom, never grew fond of gamey duck meat with dark pellet holes through it.

Dad demonstrated a more creative use for his new shotgun—his annual practice of shooting the top off a prize pine or spruce for our Christmas tree. While driving to the woods in search of a tree, he'd usually sing. He had a good tenor voice but he was too shy to join the church choir. A line from one of his favorite songs was, "There is power, power, wonder-working power, in the blood of the Lamb." For the longest time, a key word remained a mystery to me. I thought the word was "land" not "lamb" and I wondered about the source of all the blood. It wasn't until my early teens, during my confirmation class at church, that it became clear to me. "Lamb" referred to Jesus and I understood he spilled his blood for us on the cross without fighting back.

DAD'S SACRED CHRISTMAS RITUAL

Mom wanted us to be ushers at church, and I remember how, for a year or two, we begrudgingly complied. We had to lead people to pews and hand out programs for the service. We also passed plates full of chopped up pieces of the "body of Christ" down the aisles, followed by little individual shot glasses of His blood. No one drank from the same glass in the United Church. We believed in sanitary sanctity.

One Sunday morning, I looked into the church kitchen to see Mrs. Howey pouring Welch's Grape Juice into those containers and Mrs. Warren cutting up slices of Wonder Bread—the cheapest white bread you could buy. It seemed sacrilegious to me that the ingredients of this sacred ritual could be purchased by anyone at Freiburger's Grocery.

Dad seldom talked about religion. It was a private matter for him, just like voting. He only expressed passion for his business, fishing and hunting, and, in a reserved manner, for his family. He and his brothers, along with a few friends and employees, would head off every mid-November to the forests of Eastern Ontario to hunt deer. They'd usually come back at the end of the week with a dozen or so stiff, half-frozen carcasses. I witnessed, and later helped with, the ritual of hanging them from the factory rafters, skinning, and cutting them up. This would result in our required chewing of some pretty tough and stringy venison, which Mom felt obliged to store in our freezer for occasional meals. She preferred beef or pork but humored Dad in his cherished blood sports.

At age 15, I was old enough to purchase a deer hunting license and join the annual hunt. This involved staying in a cold rustic shack where we cooked and ate, and where men traded well-lubricated stories about past hunting exploits, like the year they all bagged a deer on the first three days and had to hold their fire for the rest of the week because one deer per hunter was all that was allowed.

For the hunt that year, Dad let me use his old Lee-Enfield .303, a repeat-action manual loading rifle used in World War II. On the first morning, he placed me in the middle of a field on a large rock—a peaceful spot to be on a sunny November day with a sprinkling of snow on the ground. He walked off toward a hill and into the woods to await the hunting dogs. I stretched out against the rock and started to doze a bit. Suddenly, the braying of our hounds woke me from my daydream. I looked up as a large doe appeared on the hillside before me, about 100 yards (91.5 meters) away. She froze, trying to determine her next best move.

My rifle rested solidly on the rock in the right direction and, almost by reflex, I took aim and pulled the trigger—a mechanical action. The deer seemed to flinch and then took off. The hunting dogs suddenly emerged from the forest and followed the scent.

As I walked up the hill toward the action, I saw Uncle Gerald approaching. He had been bringing up the hounds.

"I guess I missed it," I offered apologetically, but he shook his head.

"No, see the blood?"

We could easily follow the dark red trail in the brown leaves and snow. We came to a gulley and saw the doe lying there—dogs swarming her, but trained not to bite into the flesh. We dragged her carcass into the open, ready to be picked up later by Gerald driving a small tractor and wagon used for the purpose.

At lunch, the men treated me to a ritual toast of sweet red wine and slaps on the back for being the first person in the gang to bag a deer that year. I could see my dad, who sipped a little wine for the occasion, was really proud of me for my perfect shot. But it seemed all too easy to me.

After lunch, we went out to hunt again. One of the men told me to stay in a small clearing, part way up a hill crowned by a large rock. A bone-chilling wind had blown in from the northwest. My feet and hands started to freeze. I heard the hounds coming closer, then the sounds of rustling in bushes, pounding on the frozen ground, and labored breathing. A medium-size buck leapt out of the woods and up the hill. I fired as it jumped over me, but missed. I tried to load another bullet into the chamber. It jammed for an instant. I pulled the lever back, and then forward once more. The bullet slid in and I swung the rifle and fired again. The buck dropped on top of the rock a short distance away. Blood oozed from its neck.

Uncle Archie appeared from the woods to say, "Great going, Neill. I saw your second shot."

"Thanks," I mumbled, through the sputtering and gurgling of the gruesome and painful death I had caused. My stomach churned and I vomited on a patch of snow.

Archie finished the buck off with a bullet to the brain, and the woods fell silent as we dragged its carcass to a trail, ready to be picked up later.

That evening the men poured me one more glass of sweet red wine and I received more man-to-man, ritualistic pats on the back. I'd bagged the only two deer of the hunt so far.

I played the game well the rest of the week, but I didn't shoot any more deer and, to this day, have never fired a gun again.

MY GREAT-GREAT GRANDFATHER
WILLIAM MCKEE'S TOMBSTONE

6

Final Departures

I never thought for a minute about committing suicide or anything so dramatic as a way of leaving Elmira. But there did seem to me to be a lot of deaths in our family before I came into the world, and even more during my childhood—final departures, so to speak. Grandpa McKee was killed in that farm accident 12 years before I was born, and Grandpa Neill had died of a stroke when I was only a toddler. Mom told me I once sat on his knee, but I can't remember him at all.

Almost every time we went through the Village of Glen Allan on our way to Uncle John's farm, Dad would stop at the cemetery behind a church to show us the tombstones of his father and other McKee ancestors. To Dad, these tombstones were not scary at all. They were a natural part of the valley he grew up in—reminders of our family's departed souls. The stories they told were interwoven with the coming and melting of snow, the planting and sprouting of oats and wheat, the full fields of hot summers, and the tall stooks of autumn harvests.

One day in early 1952, Dad took Mom to the hospital to have another baby, and then returned home to look after us kids. During the night, the phone rang and we all woke up to gather around. I saw the look on Dad's face as he repeated the word "died." Karen started to cry, thinking Mom had died. This set off the same reaction in Glen and me, filling the room with sobs. Dad hung up and told us the baby, a girl, had died, not our mom.

Beverley, as my parents named her posthumously, briefly came into the world with "a hole in her heart." No one explained to me what that meant. They arranged for her burial in Elmira's Union Cemetery, installing a small stone marker to show her place of rest.

However, our parents believed in celebrating life and not looking backwards, as soon became obvious. About a year later, Mom gave birth to twins: a girl, Frances, and a boy, Philip. Mom claimed, "God gave us double payback for the loss of Beverley."

Despite the successful birth of the twins in our immediate family, death continued to stalk our extended family. In 1955, after Grandma Neill moved in with us, the boom of a crane came crashing down on the head of her sixth son, Uncle Gerald Neill, in an industrial accident in Kitchener. He died instantly. I knew by then that Grandma Neill had experienced a lot of tragedy in her life and I think maybe that's why she didn't like talk of guns and shooting people. Mom told us her eldest sister, Eleanor, had died as

OUR FAMILY IN 1953, WITH ME ON THE LEFT,
SORT OF SLOUCHING.

a teenager in the big flu epidemic of 1918, two years
before Mom was born.

By the time I was eight, I had also learned about
Grandma's fifth son, my Uncle Addison Neill. In 1949,
he perished in a plane crash in northern Manitoba
while returning from a two-year assignment as a
radio operator at Clyde River on the northeast coast
of Baffin Island. [That's about all I was told at the
time, but when writing this book, I searched for more
details. Uncle Addison had been helping to monitor
radio signals and flights in the Arctic—protecting us

all from a surprise attack by the Soviet Union. His Royal Canadian Airforce plane crashed into a rise of land to the east of Norway House. According to the *Winnipeg Free Press*, August 24, 1949, "all 21 persons aboard their amphibious Canso airplane perished in the crash." The paper gave an eyewitness account of the wreckage with photos of the burned-out plane and the 600 by 60-foot (183 by 18-meter) "swatch it cut through a 'neck' of rugged forested terrain. The plane was flying low, evidently trying to avoid a dangerous lightning storm." The article described scattered and battered airplane parts, luggage, and bodies, including those of "seven poor little Eskimo kids being flown out as polio victims from a mysterious outbreak in their igloos in the north." A sidebar titled "Victim's twin boys" began, "Still too stunned to cry, the attractive Doreen Neill sat on the veranda at her home in this Middlesex County village Wednesday night and watched her eight-year-old twins tussling for possession of a toy auto."] The paper had it wrong. They were seven at the time.

Uncle Addison left behind Aunt Doreen and, from oldest to youngest: John, the twins David and Alec, and Richard. Most of the Arctic carvings, and other presents Uncle Addison had collected for his wife and boys, lay shattered on the frozen ground, lost forever.

This is when my double first cousins entered my life. Aunt Doreen, my father's older sister, was an attractive, smart, and practical woman. After a short period of mourning, she moved her family from Glencoe to Elmira, where she put a down-payment on a big house on Riverside Drive. Grandma McKee moved in to help her daughter raise her four boys. Doreen took a job as a

AUNT DOREEN AND, LEFT TO RIGHT:
ALEC, RICHARD, DAVID, JOHN

Singer sewing machine saleslady. She also excelled as a seamstress, making clothes for others. She had to work hard to make money because she received very little compensation from the Canadian government for her husband's tragic death.

Richard fell between Glen and me in age and became like a real brother to us. We even made small cuts on our arms and put them together to become actual blood brothers. We played with Richard along the Canagagigue Creek, down the hill from his house. We all dressed in similar colorful striped jerseys. Our hair was short, brush cut style, but usually matted down. We only had to take full baths on Saturday nights or when we got really filthy.

Richard would also come to our neighborhood, a place which offered a wider range of movement through fields around the factories. We'd sometimes sneak into a municipal yard to play in an enormous pile of sand used for spreading on slippery roads in winter. We'd climb to the top and slide down, setting off small landslides, which partially buried us.

Richard shared his comic books with us, as well as those of his older brothers. I still liked *Archie* the best, and Westerns like *Ringo Kid*, but I didn't care for *Superman*. I'd already tried parachuting off our garage roof and knew I'd never be able to fly, so why should I pretend I could?

Richard had a paper route to earn pocket money and we sometimes helped him. We would use our allowances to treat one another to bubble gum and "long john" cream puffs, jaw breakers, and comic wax teeth and lips—even long black licorice twists to use as whips before we ate them, and then we'd show off who had the blackest teeth. A store in a small house a few doors down from Richard's place sold all of these delights to neighborhood kids, making both of the dentists in town richer and richer.

With Richard and other kids, I spent hours trading baseball cards decked with pictures of heroes I really didn't know. Dad never watched sports on our new TV and I preferred action programs, like cowboy movies, not this slow-motion stuff with complicated rules that made the players stop all the time. Of course, ice hockey was okay—a very fast game. I also liked playing games with many-colored marbles, which I carried in cloth bags that made my pockets bulge, like a rich man, and they rattled when I ran. I'd have to shift my pocket knife, yo-yo, coins, shiny stones, or other cool stuff I'd found, to the opposite side pocket for counter-balance.

Richard sometimes joined us on our exploration of the Canagagigue Creek, though he was more cautious. Feeling sad for him that he had lost his father, we never teased him like his older brothers did. We explored all parts of Richard's house, including the basement where, for some reason, a former owner had installed a urinal on the wall so he didn't have to go upstairs to pee. Its once-white porcelain had turned a rusty color but it still worked well for us.

Aunt Doreen encouraged her sons to learn new things—to experiment. Richard's older brother David (the one who had identified the ostrich poop in our neighborhood a few years before, and taught us how to avoid getting "buggered" on the creek), kept his chemistry set in the basement. I loved the different names of the acids and elements he showed us, and I would watch

THE LAB OF MY GENIUS COUSIN

83

with amazement when he mixed them together to turn different colors, bubble-up, and stink.

As David advanced in age, he advanced in his chemistry skills as well. He learned how to make beer and distill liquor in the basement. But for me, the highlight of his early chemistry career came when he and a friend made a bomb. They set off this experimental device down by the creek and the explosion echoed throughout town. Fire alarms sounded. People called in to see if the chemical plant had blown up.

David and his friend had wisely taken cover before their bomb went off, and so they escaped without injury. He told me later he didn't return home directly, but when he did, he must have had a smirk on his face for Aunt Doreen forbade him to use his chemistry set, at least for a while. I marveled at how he managed to pull off this trick without severe punishment from his mother or being reported to the police.

On Halloween one year, David and Alec, with some of their friends, started a fire in the drainage tunnel that ran through town, causing the firetruck to come. What better way to have a volunteer fire department stay in shape without doing any real harm? (I suppose Norman and I carried out a more dangerous operation when we set fire to the field beside the shirt and overall factory, though we hadn't planned our blaze.)

We never did any real damage on Halloween. We put on simple costumes and tried to keep up with Richard's older brothers by covering as much territory in the trick-or-treat game as possible, seeing who could be first to fill a shopping bag with treats, then taking it home and spreading them out on the floor to make trades. Our parents never accompanied us on these neighborhood gathering expeditions. Everyone considered the town safe and juvenile pranks were expected.

We all experienced a childhood of freedom. We could go just about anywhere, exploring the town and surrounding countryside. In the summer, we swam naked at what we dubbed the "BAB," code for "bare ass beach." This natural facility lay on the bank of Larch's Creek, a tributary of the Canagagigue—fortunately upstream from Naugatuck Chemicals. But we had to share our swimming hole with a herd of cattle. Considering all the run-off of manure from the fields, plus the cows' direct deposits in the creek, I don't know how we escaped getting diseases. I guess our immune systems had become very strong because of all the kinds of dirt we played in.

One summer's day when we were swimming at the BAB with my little dog Peggy, the cattle came toward us, probably attracted by the dog but possibly offended by

I DON'T REMEMBER PRECISELY, BUT THAT'S
PROBABLY ALEC IN THE CREEK.

our prolonged occupation of their drinking and bathing place. They advanced like a line of soldiers in a medieval war, horns at the ready, and we had to give up the territory for the day.

Although Aunt Doreen gave her boys a free pass to roam about, I found her to be strict in other ways. She didn't believe in Santa Claus and so Richard never experienced Christmas the way we did. As a struggling single mom, she didn't have money for many presents. She also had strong opinions like her mother, Grandma McKee, and didn't believe one should keep up the hoax about Santa Claus. When I was a toddler, Grandma McKee shoved tomatoes into my mouth at a family picnic, trying to make me like them. I never forgave her for that. I tried to avoid both Doreen and Grandma as much as possible while playing at Richard's place.

At least Aunt Doreen encouraged her sons to read. She read a book a day, even with all her work. She volunteered at the town's library and that gave her special access. But I figured she read too much because, one winter's day, she gathered up her boys' whole comic book collection and threw it into their coal furnace. She didn't approve of adolescents reading such material. [Perhaps she had been reading books by an American psychiatrist, Dr. Wertham, who in the 1950s campaigned against comic books, claiming they encouraged sexual and criminal activity by young people.] It's true *Archie* comics had a lot on Archie's attraction to girls. That's probably why I liked them so much.

It was a sad day for all of us when the comic book collection suddenly disappeared. How could we learn anything useful? I found my school books dreadfully

ARCHIE AND HIS LATEST GIRLFRIEND BURNING IN HELL

boring. I got a library card but I couldn't find any comic books there. The kids' section consisted of silly stories about prissy girls or lessons on how to be good. The adventure books on cowboys were non-violent, so I didn't believe them—pure propaganda.

Even without comic books, Richard maintained his wild imagination—big words would come out of his brain. He could also add, subtract, multiply, and divide in his head. He was short and skinny and usually remained quiet around adults, even shy. But he had no problem in asking, "What are you having?" when invited to stay for supper. He would call home to compare menus before accepting.

As it turned out, unlike my mom who gave birth to twins a year after losing Beverley, Aunt Doreen never received payback from God for the death of her husband. As she drove out of town on an icy Saturday morning in April 1956, she lost control and swerved into an oncoming car in the opposite lane. She died instantly from severe internal injuries. Cousin Alec, seated in the back seat, broke his leg. The impact caused Doreen's friend, Mrs. Backes, to be ejected from the passenger seat onto the road. She alone escaped serious injury.

That morning, as I watched a cowboy program on TV, which involved sending an urgent telegram, Dad came rushing in and called, "Alma! Alma! Doreen's been killed!"

Our family came together in the kitchen to listen to the details, weep, discuss the tragedy, and decide on the need to send a telegram to one of my mother's brothers, John Neill in Vancouver. I listened to all this, seated on the kitchen counter. Suddenly I blurted out a possible message in a staccato, monotone voice: "DOREEN KILLED IN CAR ACCIDENT. STOP."

Mom rebuked me, "Neill, stop that. We don't need your two cents. Your aunt's been killed."

My face grew hot and I started to cry, then suddenly bolted upstairs to my room. The next day, Dad took Glen and me to see our aunt's crushed Studebaker. I still remember its mangled and blood-stained steering wheel, which had bashed into her chest. That's when I learned for certain that death involved more than just telling stories.

A few days later, my parents took us to Dreisinger's funeral parlor, where I saw my first dead body. I wondered if my parents wanted to punish me for my dumb comment about the telegram. Aunt Doreen somehow looked so beautiful in the casket, as if she were still alive, and I couldn't reconcile this with the bloody steering wheel. I wanted to tell her how sorry I was for what I had said, but I knew I couldn't take back my stupid "telegram" words.

I saw Richard at the funeral, but soon afterwards he too vanished from our lives. The family decided to send him to Vancouver to live with Uncle John Neill, a professor of horticulture at the University of British Columbia. Richard joined Uncle John, Aunt Ona, and our cousin Catharine. I had not foreseen Richard's sudden disappearance. For the first time, I realized death has real consequences. I wanted to go with him.

Much to my surprise, we did get to see Richard the following summer, after we visited the Calgary Stampede. We crossed the Rocky Mountains in a train with observation cars, gliding along like a great snake. I had only dreamed about what I saw—gray peaks poking through the clouds, tunnels carved through walls of rock, swift rivers, high waterfalls, vast forests, and small towns tucked into green valleys. But when we reached Vancouver, I found it to be an anti-climax. Richard didn't seem the same. I noticed how in his new family he had little freedom to fool around with us. I saw that Aunt Ona insisted he keep his clothes clean. She kept a close eye on him. He'd been tamed.

Our double first cousin and blood brother had left us for a different world, thousands of miles away—in a way, another final departure.

RICHARD, THE SHORTEST GUY,
WITH HIS NEW FAMILY AND GLEN AND ME.

7
Breaking Out

When our orphaned cousin Richard left Elmira, Glen and I were lucky to have another close cousin our age: Lenny. Mom loved to take us to her older sister Elsie McCurdy's place in Streetsville, not far from Toronto. Aunt Elsie had been a school teacher until she got married in 1937, when, according to the rules in Ontario at the time, she had to quit. She also taught Sunday school and Mom always looked up to her. We didn't mind going to Streetsville because we really liked Lenny, and—to me—his town smelled completely different from Elmira.

In fact, we went to Streetsville for a week every summer and Lenny came to Elmira before or after that—kind of a back-to-back vacation exchange. Lenny liked to explore our creeks and rivers with Glen and me, but what impressed him most was our dad's factory: metal cutters crashing, lathes humming, welders buzzing, and

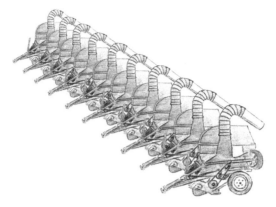

MCKEE MODEL-D HARVESTERS, READY FOR SHIPMENT

assembly line pounding, bang, bang, bang. The three of us inspected the factory yard full of bright red and yellow hay harvesters, all lined up for shipment. Glen and I proudly showed Lenny all the parts being made and put together—the complicated business our dad and his brother had achieved with only eighth-grade educations. By the mid-1950s, they employed about 50 people and had dealers selling their machines across Canada and in some U.S. states.

When we went to Streetsville, Lenny revealed to us his different world. We explored the nearby Credit River, which flows into Lake Ontario. We inspected Uncle Wilbert's used car sales lot, various factories, the railway station and tracks—a much busier rail line than the two in Elmira. For the first time before falling asleep, I heard the lonely sound of train whistles in the night.

I noticed that Lenny displayed salesman tendencies from the start. Rather than selling lemonade on the street, he showed us how to salvage and resell things. One time, a window production company's dumpster provided us with a load of scrap wood, which we carted home to Lenny's place. I can't recall if our original plan was to sell it, but later that day when Aunt Elsie left us to our own devices, we built a whole room-like structure in the basement, nailing it firmly onto the bare ceiling rafters, which seemed to be crying out for completion.

When Uncle Wilbert, who walked and talked at a snail's pace, came home in the evening, he poked around at what we'd done. I could see his face getting red and wondered if he would blow up, but he stepped back and looked real serious, saying, "Well, you boys will need to take apart your handiwork tomorrow."

I thought I saw one side of his mouth slide up in a smile, and I sensed a real appreciation for our project. Like our dad, Uncle Wilbert had been born and raised on a farm and worked with his hands from an early age. Until then, he must have thought we'd been lacking such experience. But we really showed him!

As we grew older, we grew bolder in Streetsville. Near the end of our final summer visit, our creative experimentation included the different spit patterns we could deliver from a railway bridge onto the wind-shields of vehicles passing below. This "art work" ended when a car screeched to a halt and a tall man came running up the concrete steps to the tracks. We had little time to get away.

"Head for the railway shed," Lenny said. "Don't look back." We dashed and dove behind it.

"Did he see us? I asked.

"Shhhhssss," Glen motioned toward the invisible man.

"What can he do to us?" I whispered.

Lenny and Glen didn't answer. We stood there frozen

THOU SHALT NOT SPIT FROM A BRIDGE!

for a minute. Then the suspense got to me and I stupidly stuck my head out to check. The man grabbed me by the front of my shirt.

"You broke my windshield, you little buggers!"

"No sir, that's impossible," Lenny protested. Glen nodded.

I also knew he had to be mistaken because our chosen media of expression had been saliva on glass, not stones on glass. Evidently, falling saliva meeting a speeding windshield looks like cracks on glass, but the guy wouldn't let up. He pulled me by the left ear, and then turned to Glen and Lenny. "You guys come with me too."

"Where're you taking us?" Glen asked.

"You'll see."

We went down the stairs to his car and he made us stand there. Just then, a police car came by and stopped to investigate. Panic caused my brain to shut down. All I can remember is the three of us lined up in the back seat of the cruiser, headed for jail.

The cop didn't say much. He asked for our address so Lenny told him, and that's where he took us, much to our relief. When we got to Lenny's house, he warned us severely in front of Aunt Elsie.

When he finally departed, Aunt Elsie picked up where he'd left off. The only new thing I heard from the policeman was that railway tracks are private property and we'd been trespassing. This seemed questionable to me because I knew every inch of the train tracks around Elmira and no one ever bothered me, Glen, and our friends, when we walked on them for miles. It was safe, too, as long as we got off before trains came rumbling through. We usually scrunched down behind scrub bushes as they passed—part of the fun—but I think the engineers knew we were there.

When Uncle Wilbert came home and heard the story, standing there in the middle of the living room with us boys seated quietly on the sofa, acting like we were reading our comic books, I thought I could see a slight smile on his face this time as well. I figured his childhood in the countryside must have involved exploring train tracks, too. Then he shook his head and sat down in his armchair to read the newspaper and smoke his cigarettes from a pack, which he always kept in his shirt pocket. Seeing no further drama coming, we took our comics to the backyard until Aunt Elsie called us for supper.

When our parents came to get us on Sunday, they didn't scold us either. Instead, on the way home they stopped by the reform school for boys near Guelph.

Mom said, "This is where young boys have to live if they break the law. They learn trades like carpentry and making license plates for cars. They're given porridge for breakfast, Spam and bread at lunch, and only cold meat with potatoes and vegetables all mushed together for supper—no choices at all."

From outside, the place looked so beautiful. I could see a pond with a fountain at the entrance gate. Surely Mom exaggerated for effect.

Then Dad continued the lesson: "The boys are watched all the time by men with big sticks and guns. At night, they have to sleep behind bars. A siren wakes them up at five o'clock and they're marched out to do exercises in the yard before breakfast, even in the snow during winter. Day after day, that's their routine."

I must admit their strategy had a mildly positive effect for a while, and those vivid images remain etched in my brain to this day.

Perhaps the "saliva art" incident soured our love for going to Lenny's. One Saturday after that, when Dad was away on a business trip, Mom decided to take all of us to Streetsville for some function at Aunt Elsie's church. Glen and I had started arguing against this trip the day before and continued during breakfast. We really wanted to take our bicycles out into the countryside to fish with some friends. For kids our age, we were pretty good at arguing, and so we continued making our case every which way we could.

We had only reached the West Montrose covered bridge on the Grand River, about four miles (6.5 km) outside of Elmira, when Mom stopped the car and yelled, "Get out! You can walk home!"

Glen and I dutifully exited the car and stood there. She slammed the door and drove off with Karen and our twin brother and sister, Philip and Frances. The car grew smaller and disappeared around a corner.

I looked at Glen and said, "Just wait, she'll come back. It's only a warning." But we stood there in silence for about ten minutes before we realized she wouldn't be returning.

On the long trek home, Glen and I remained silent most of the way. We bickered a little over who said what to Mom to cause her outburst. Usually, she could take our arguing. We'd never seen her blow up like that. We had our reasons for resisting the trip to Streetsville so soon after being "arrested" by the policeman. Going back to the scene of the crime didn't sound like a smart thing to do. Besides, the church event would have been unbearably dreary and we thought Lenny would understand. Maybe he would escape it as well, if we didn't show up.

Although it was mid-September, the sun beat down relentlessly on our heads. It took us ages to reach our house—never locked in those days. We arrived all sweaty and worn out, too late to go anywhere, our strategy a total failure.

As an alternative to unsupervised roaming around our towns in the summer, Mom and Aunt Elsie had started to register us in the United Church Boys' Camp on Lake Huron. I think they wanted to program us—keep our little minds and hands busy with religion and whole-some sports and crafts.

The last year we attended the camp—probably our third year in a row—we already knew the routine: racing, playing softball, hiking, and improving swimming skills; pretending to be Indians by carving wooden totem poles and sewing beads onto leather; mumbling prayers at meals; and singing the same old hymns and camp songs by the fireside every evening. For me, the highlight of each day was buying chocolate bars and other sweet snacks in mid-afternoon at what was called the "tuck shop."

One evening, a kid in our cabin of ten boys, called "Busy Beavers," pointed out the distant lights of the beach arcade at Port Elgin. It could have been Lenny who first had the idea, but I have no exact memory or proof. Anyway, we began to plan a breakout. We'd head to Port Elgin to play on the pinball machines.

After evening campfire, all campers and counselors gathered in the mess hall to cross our arms in front and hold hands while we sang a song set to the tune of "Taps"—one that most knew by heart:

Day is done,
gone the sun,
from the lake,
from the hills,
from the sky;
All is well,
safely rest,
God is nigh.

At the end of the song, we all had to shout, "Thanks for the evening, partners!"

On the last evening, after this final gesture of thanks, the ten of us broke the circle by forcefully pushing down while letting go of the hands we were holding, and then rushing out the door into the dark. Our good planning led to precise execution. We dashed down the road and into the dark woods along the shoreline. We could see the lights of Port Elgin through the trees, but had resolved to lay low until we had a chance to make a break for it.

In the distance, we could hear the camp counselors, totally caught off guard, starting to organize, shouting out orders and getting into cars. Some sped off down the road. Others advanced on foot into the woods with flashlights, yelling, "Busy Beavers, we know you're there. You'd better surrender!"

We hugged the ground, frozen in small groups. But one of the boys was wearing a beige jacket, which reflected too much moonlight. They caught him with two others. Three more made a break for the beach, but counselors intercepted them. Another counselor shouted, "We've got six of you Beavers. The rest of you have two minutes to surrender or we'll call the police. You'll go to reform school."

With such a threat, the last group, including Lenny, Glen, a guy named Charlie, and me, decided to give up. I don't think any of us really intended to reach Port Elgin. We didn't have much money to play pinball anyway. I'd already spent most of my camp allowance on tuck shop. But at least we had succeeded in performing a clean breakout.

After a predictable lecture from the camp director, we were assigned an extra counselor to sleep in our cabin that night. They also watched us closely the next morning, escorting us to and from breakfast and lunch. In between, they kept us in our cabin and stood guard, even accompanying us when we had to take a pee.

When Mom and Aunt Elsie arrived in the afternoon, the camp director briefed them on our crime; then they also scolded us and told us we had been banned by the camp authorities, forever.

We all remained silent as Mom drove toward Elmira, where Aunt Elsie had parked her car. Perhaps our mothers drifted into the realm of self-blame, wondering where they had failed as parents. I briefly felt a little sorry for them that they had sons like us who didn't care much about churchy things. Their father had been a United Church minister and Mom often said she hoped Glen or I would become one too. Actually, I think I felt more pity for Mom and Aunt Elsie because they thought being banned from church camp was punishment.

I can't say we learned any great lesson from these escapades with Lenny. Our parents' troubles with us were far from over, but at least I can proudly report none of us ever had to break out of reform school or prison. [Lenny eventually became a super computer entrepreneur and multi-millionaire, and as for Glen and me, you'll have to keep reading.]

BREAKING OUT!

MY NEW ROCKET

8

Perpetual Motion

Throughout my childhood, I gradually became more and more sophisticated in preventing the town's odors from entering my nostrils, through the theory and practice of perpetual motion. A full understanding of this requires returning, once again, to my early years.

A first taste of this kind of freedom came when we graduated from trashy bicycles. Dad took Glen and me to Lorne Martin's Central Cycle & Sports store to buy our first brand new bicycles. (We called him "Horny Lornie" but never to his face.) They were made by Canada Cycle & Motor Co. Ltd. and known as "CCMs," the only kind to have according to the kids in school. I chose blue and Glen chose red—different colors so there'd be no arguments on which one belonged to whom. These vehicles allowed us to fly like rockets, round corners on dangerous slants, jump over potholes in the road, and head into unknown territory.

We'd compete with each other and our friends on who could drive the longest without hands on the handlebars, shouting at pedestrians, "Look, no hands!" Once in a while our daredevil antics would lead to disaster. My comeuppance came one summer's day as I rounded a sharp corner at high speed, hit some loose gravel, and went flying. I had to pick the stones out of my wounded knee and wind my handkerchief around it, hobbling to our house with a now disabled rocket, handlebars pushed out of shape. When I reached home, Mom flew into action with hot water and soap, followed by stinging iodine, which made it hurt a lot more. In a few days, a large brown scab formed on my knee—kind of a trophy to show the other guys.

For the sound of a motor, we used clothespins to fasten cardboard separators from Shredded Wheat boxes to the front fender braces, extending them into the spokes so they would flap. The faster you drove the more racket you could make. People turned their heads and frowned at us. One time an old geezer with a cane raised his weapon at me, ready to fight the invader of his peaceful stroll. But in my mind, I flew by so fast I figured he'd never identify me. You had to be careful in a small town. Everybody knew everybody. We could push the limits only so far, or phone calls would be made to our parents and our bicycles confiscated for a week—like a jail sentence.

In fairness to Elmira, sugar maples, elms, oaks, chestnuts, and evergreens lined many streets, absorbing some of the stinks, and providing welcome shelter from sudden showers and mid-summer sun. In autumn, most people raked falling leaves to the curbsides and set them on fire. These bonfires added a kind of pleasant burnt offering to the air, reminding us that the cleansing snow would soon be falling. We drove our new bicycles at high speed, right through these fires, spreading burning ashes onto the sidewalk.

The longest and steepest hill in town was on nearby Erb Street, where Ricky Woods lived. His street came to a dead end at the entrance to the chemical factory. Ricky had been stricken with cerebral palsy in his early child-hood, and he walked with the aid of metal leg braces. At the time we got to know him, Glen and I were mak-ing soapboxes out of scrap plywood from our dad's nearby warehouse. We created these four-wheel rock-ets and painted them in bright yellow with red flames.

TRYING OUT THE STEEPEST HILL IN TOWN

For wheels, we had to be satisfied with what we could salvage from old baby buggies and wagons in the town dump, or from Conrad's junk yard. We mounted the front wheels on a narrow board that swiveled by pulling ropes tied on each side. The driver had to hold them taut for control. Ricky provided commentary on our progress and added calculations, using the formula, momentum = mass x velocity.

One day, on his insistence, we helped Ricky—metal leg braces and all—into one of our latest creations. We bade him good luck and gave him a starting push. As we stood watching from the top of the hill, Ricky's mass added to that of the soapbox, and descended with such an alarming velocity that the momentum they generated gave me goosebumps, while my brother clutched his head in a futile attempt to protect Ricky's skull. This was long before kids wore helmets.

Ricky's planned course included a sharp turn to the left down a small lane at the bottom of the hill. But somehow our contraption got hooked to a guy-wire connected to a pole beside the entrance to the factory. The soapbox stopped abruptly, upended, and Ricky shot out. We ran down the hill to his rescue, hoping his mother had not witnessed our experiment. By the time we reached the scene, Ricky was dusting himself off.

I said, "Holy cow, Ricky, you alright?"

Barely shaken, he looked up at us and beamed, "Can I do it again?"

We didn't talk about the disaster too much. [But many years later, my brother ran into Ricky, who still spoke of the thrill of that day. In spite of his handicap, he had graduated in mathematics and had become a teacher at a nearby college. When I heard this, I thought, *Who could dispute the value of our physics experiment and its social benefit?*]

Access to Dad's factory gave us tools and equipment few boys possessed. We soon upgraded our soapbox efforts to motorized go-carts, motivated by the occasional visit with Dad to stockcar races, where we breathed in the intoxicating fumes of high-octane racing fuel mixed with the stink of rubber burning on asphalt. Paul Martin assisted us with these early motorized efforts. He was older than us—old enough to drive—but he would forever be limited to riding around on a bicycle because he suffered from epilepsy. He knew he would never have a driver's license because of his condition, so our go-carts represented partial compensation for him. Glen encouraged him in this business, taking special precautions to prevent his having an accident. It seemed to me my brother always liked to help less fortunate guys. Paul's older brother, aware of our shenanigans and Paul's limitations, instructed Glen on how to stick a ruler in his mouth to prevent him from chewing his tongue when he had a strong fit.

From an early age, Glen and I had gradually explored every corner of the McKee Brothers factory and yard, using this great space on weekends for learning about motion, machines, and mechanics—exhilarating escapes into a fast-paced world. By the time we were 11 or 12, we had learned to speed the company's lift tractor and battered old army jeep around lines of bright red and yellow harvesters. We knew the jeep had been purchased from Canadian Army surplus, a fact which added to its allure. I imagined myself in the front lines of World War II as I maneuvered it through tight spaces, working its worn steel brake and clutch pedals, while quickly shifting gears just at the right time.

It wasn't long before I also tried motorized propulsion on water, inspired by the air-powered contraption Uncle Jim had taken fishing on Lake Nipissing. I acquired a small airplane motor with a propeller. I worked through an entire winter building a wooden flat-bottomed boat and sealing it with fiberglass. In the spring, when I took it to the creek for a trial, it barely floated and moved along the water at a snail's pace. In great disappointment, I junked the thing. I should have involved Ricky Woods in doing some calculations on momentum = mass x velocity.

I did better in building two-wheel land vehicles, thanks to Glen's help. I think we became inspired when Dad took us to the nearby Heidelberg motorcycle climb to see daredevils flying up a steep hill with powerful Triumphs, Indians, and Harleys.

After viewing such spectacular feats, Glen and I bought some old bicycles, removed the back wheels, and modified the frames by welding on steel boxes, which we cut and formed with the factory's metal-working machines. On the bottom of each box, we mounted bearings and an axle with an airplane wheel. Our motorbikes were powered by one- or two-horsepower Briggs & Stratton gasoline motors, which we bolted to the top of the box. A centrifugal force pulley on the motor gradually tightened a V-belt as we throttled up, providing power to a countershaft that drove the airplane wheel by a chain and sprocket system.

At our age, we couldn't apply for drivers' licenses, and we never even tried to acquire license plates for our homemade motorbikes. They could reach at least 25 miles (40 km) an hour, but they were only equipped with regular front-wheel bicycle brakes—pads that pressed on the front wheel rim. The brakes didn't work very well. For faster stops, we had to drag our feet on the ground.

In town, we mainly stuck to the streets near our house or Dad's factory. I recall flying by Constable Wheeler, out for an evening stroll with his dog. He waved frantically, signaling us to stop. But we simply waved back at him and kept on going. For some reason, we never got caught, though we sometimes took these contraptions on the sideroads out of town, far into the countryside. We strapped on tanks of extra gasoline and made it as far as Uncle John's farm, 15 miles (24 km) from Elmira.

Dad never stopped us from taking such trips. We were blessed by his encouragement and he never directed us on exactly what to do. He just smiled and told us to

MY MARVELOUS MOTORBIKE

DAD'S CAR-TRACTOR HYBRID

be careful. He must have thought it best for children to experiment and learn by themselves.

Many years later, my cousin Kenneth, who still lives on the farm where Dad grew up, sent me an old faded photo of Dad on a Model-T car he had converted into a tractor when he was in his teens. When I saw the photo, I finally understood why Dad supported and encouraged our experiments in perpetual motion.

9

Proving Ground

Glen and I had to work from an early age—no free ride in the McKee household. We suffered under what I would call "a regime of indentured child labor with the smallest of rewards." But this money did give us an ever-increasing freedom of choice and movement.

Our first job, at ages five and six, involved carrying a blue and yellow honey pail of food scraps every day from our house to a pack of hungry hunting hounds kept in a pen outside Dad and Uncle Gerald's first shop in the center of town. We would hum songs together as we walked along to the dogs' jail, holding the pail between us. I think the humming built our courage.

These poor dogs only got to go hunting four or five times a year. Otherwise, no one paid much attention to them on a daily basis, besides us. When we approached the hole in the wire mesh, they'd gnash their teeth and growl at each other to gain greater shares of the scraps. We took turns guardedly pouring their food in, afraid they'd chomp our fingers too. For this task, we received an allowance of ten cents a week, an amount which rose to possibly as much as 15 cents after a couple of years. Dad said he'd started at 15 cents an hour as a machine shop assistant in his late teens, so how could we complain?

Like most kids, we also had other routine jobs, like taking out the garbage, and some seasonal work as well. In the summer, we had to mow the lawn and hoe the garden. At about age 11 and 12, we started earning real money in the summers by working with carpenters, assembling hay wagons at McKee Brothers warehouse, located to the west of the shirt and overall factory near the willow tree. I loved the smell of new lumber and plywood. Sometimes we got to do spray painting. If I didn't wear a mask, I'd get a little dizzy with all the fumes—but that made me pleasantly float.

By 1959, Dad and Uncle Gerald's farm equipment business was doing even better, employing around 110 people in Elmira and had many salesmen and dealers across Canada and the U.S. They added a 200-foot extension to their factory to build their "one-man" shredder harvesters, as well as other products.

MCKEE BROTHERS' EXPANDED FACTORY

During those days, most farmer's sons were quitting farming to work in towns and factories, or to get a higher education for better paying jobs, and the McKee shredder harvester allowed one man to operate a 100- to 200-acre (40.5- to 81-hectare) property by himself, or with a son who wanted to farm. He could sell out to his son or another buyer, and retire with enough money to live on.

One of the first real jobs we had at the expanded factory was what I remember as "the Christmas lights brigade." During Christmas vacation, Glen and I had to wash many rows of fluorescent lights hanging from the factory's steel rafters. We performed this job on a scaffold about 10 feet (three meters) above the concrete floor. We had to climb down frequently and push the heavy structure forward to the next section of lights.

Our hands became red and sore because we immersed them all day in a trough of cold and increasingly dirty water. At first, we wore rubber gloves, but found the long florescent bulbs to be too slippery when wet. Once, I let a bulb slip out of my gloved hands, and I watched it explode on the floor below. I could imagine my head doing the same, like a ripe watermelon, if I ever fell. Every few hours, we changed the water by siphoning it into pails below, starting the downward flow by sucking on the hose, often getting a mouthful of grimy water in the process.

After all the employees had received their annual turkey gifts and taken off for a week-long Christmas break, we worked in relative silence and made better progress. But because of all our family's Christmas celebrations with relatives, we never could finish before the workers returned. Then, we had to quickly complete the job before school began again, all the while slaving away with clouds of black smoke and metallic dust filling our nostrils, as it rose from the welding stations below. By the time we finished all the lights, we could see a dark film of dirt accumulating on the first row we had cleaned, waiting for next season's Christmas lights brigade.

My fondest memories of my days as a child laborer don't involve factory work at all. Around age nine, I started taking private cornet lessons on Saturday mornings from Mr. Chislett, our school's music teacher. My friends said his nose had been shot off in World War II and his new one was made of plastic. I closely inspected it during my lessons instead of paying attention, so I never learned to read music. Each hour-long lesson went by as slowly as my progress.

When I was about 10, Dad announced his company had bought a farm and I faced a dilemma. I really wanted to go with him and my brother on Saturdays, so I put my problem to Mr. Chislett, "Do you think I should continue lessons?"

He quickly answered, "I think you should go to the farm." With such a ringing endorsement, my music career ended.

What Uncle Gerald and Dad called the "McKee Experimental Farm" was located about 25 miles (40 km) from Elmira on Concession Road 4 of Maryborough Township—about five miles from the McKee home farm on Concession Road 3. [I'm now convinced my father and uncle purchased this farm because they wanted to return on weekends to the valley where they were born. I don't think their business really needed it.]

The farm consisted of an old stone house and 200 acres (81 hectares) of pasture, hay, and grain crops. They added a pond and stocked it with fish for leisure time. In the summer, pasturing cattle drank and pooped at one end, so it was too filthy for swimming, except for a few wild ducks. They also built a huge pole barn with a trench silo in the middle for storing silage, thus providing green grass to the cattle all winter—a grass-fed cattle raising system much ahead of its time. I loved the sweet smell of the fresh green hay as I packed it down by running a tractor back and forth after the hay loads were blown in, using a McKee harvester. As the silage aged, it gave off a stronger but pleasant aroma, and if you dug into it, warm waves of steam rose into the air.

The company also rented another four farms—500 additional acres (202 hectares)—along the upper slopes

THE POLE BARN, STILL STANDING IN 2014

of the nearby valley, which would soon be flooded to form Lake Conestoga, a spring flood control method for the Conestoga and Grand Rivers. The Conservation Authority had purchased these farms for eventual reforestation; however, at the time they continued to provide good grazing land for a few horses and a herd of cattle.

Whether a hobby farm or not, it brought great pleasure and meaning to my dad and uncle, and it became a place for Glen and me to learn new lessons about growing up, a special kind of "proving ground."

For one thing, this land finally fulfilled my boyhood dream of becoming a cowboy. Our cousins David and Alec were put in charge of the herd of steers, and Glen and I occasionally had a chance to join them in riding the range. One time Alec, who rode the oldest horse, found his charge to be too tired to round up the cattle, so he offered it some oats he kept in a bag. The animal gorged down the delicious snack and Alec remounted, but it still wouldn't move. Apparently, he thought it should be like filling up the tank of a car with gas.

Another time, I had the opposite experience when I was ordering my horse to chase the steers for no real purpose at all. The horse, wanting to end this futility, suddenly took off at full speed down the field, heading for a fence. Right before we reached it, I pulled the reins hard, and the beast responded with such sudden and total obedience that it ejected me headfirst into the wires.

Fortunately, the fence had some spring to it, propelling me backwards onto the ground beside the horse's front hooves. Looking over at the now contented animal chomping on grass beside me, I decided I really didn't

END OF MY DREAM OF BECOMING A COWBOY

need to be a cowboy. I also learned that you can't just order horses around. As with people, they have to come to trust you first.

One summer, Glen and I stayed at the farm in our small oval-shaped trailer for a few weeks to work with the farm manager. We assisted him with cutting, raking, and harvesting hay, then packing it down in the pole barn with the tractor. The days were long. We came to appreciate what Dad and his brothers had endured as kids—and without all the machinery we had.

That same summer, the manager also gave us the job of painting a long white fence down the lane and around the front of the property. Our Tom Sawyer and Huck Finn task seemed endless. I think the manager and Dad had devised it as a means of keeping us out of trouble. But it didn't work. Glen and I began to argue. He had learned how to box, whereas I practiced the art of wrestling. One day during an argument, he started punching me. After receiving a few blows to my face from his bare fists, I grabbed him in a bear hug and pulled him down, pinning him to the ground. After I

FORMER MCKEE EXPERIMENTAL FARM IN 2014

released him, he came at me again and I simply pulled him down again. I figured that's when I finally paid Glen back for hitting me on the head with a hammer when we were younger.

The farm manager, who lived in the house with his wife, finally came to break up the fight. They had only invited us in for a few suppers. After that, they paid more attention to us. We knew they could telephone Dad and end our sojourn on the farm. So, we settled down and finished painting the fence.

The next year, the manager gave us the job of helping David and Alec bale some dry hay—a tough, dirty, sweaty job. In the afternoon of the first day, our cousins pulled out a case of cold beer at lunch break. I poured a whole bottle of the golden liquid down my throat and drank a couple more bottles as our work continued. I pleasantly floated but never really got drunk, as I quickly sweated it all out. In spite of the thick hay dust sticking to my skin, making me itchy, baling hay with this beverage was the best farm job by far. To this day, every glass of beer I drink is measured against that taste. I can still see the red baler and feel the chaff on my neck with each swallow, especially in hot weather.

On Saturday afternoons and Sundays, we didn't have to work. Glen and I had the whole valley to explore. Spring Creek, with its swimming holes and bridges, had been the playground of my dad and his siblings, and McKee generations before them. We fished from the bridge where they had fished and where our ancestors had crossed the creek for over 100 years, driving horses and carts or horse-drawn sleds in winter, to the villages of Hollen, Drayton, or Moorefield, where grain could be milled and provisions purchased.

The rented conservation land included four sets of abandoned barns and houses, which had been marked for demolition. We entered the houses to inspect traces of the families who had left only a decade ago—faded flower-patterned wallpaper, worn patches on wooden floors where chairs once stood, and pencil marks for the heights of growing children on door frames. A musty smell permeated the rooms. Mice turds covered the floors and windowsills. We avoided going into the houses alone and certainly wouldn't go to the upstairs or any secluded corner without company—too spooky.

Sometimes we amused ourselves by punching out windowpanes with our bare fists. I'd seen on some television show that if you could do it fast enough, you'd be okay. After a few successful blows, I suffered a deep cut in my right knuckle and had to wrap my hand tightly in my handkerchief to stop the bleeding.

The scar remained for many years—another lesson that I wasn't Superman.

We explored the back part of Uncle John's farm, where the McKees first built a log shanty around 1848, after arriving from Scotland. Dad had brought us to this place before. On a previous visit, he'd uncovered some shattered pottery and a few blue and white porcelain pieces.

We trudged along the remains of an old trail that used to serve as the main access road to the McKee home farm. Our ancestors helped to build it through the forest, then populated with deer, wolves, foxes, bears, and other wild animals. Dad told us a story about this road and the valley, and he managed to write it down. It had to do with his respect for our equestrian friends—a lesson I had already learned. He titled it "The Wisdom of Horses":

I think it was 1934, after our father was killed. I was only 14 at the time. We were low on coal and groceries, so I was assigned to go to Drayton, also taking a load of grain to be milled into hog feed. My brothers helped hitch up our big Clydesdale horses, Tom and Mac, for the trip. The weather was mild, although there was plenty of snow. Our neighbor next door had opened a sleigh trail across the back fields to move livestock and cattle feed. I decided to take this short cut.

The six-mile trip went well, arriving about 11 a.m. with a light snow falling. I purchased and loaded a ton of coal onto the sleigh, placing the sacks of hog feed on top, and stashing the groceries under cover, then started for home about 3:00 p.m. It was a heavy load. Normally the trip would take about two and a half hours, but within an hour it started to snow heavily with high winds. The sled tracks filled up, increasing the traction for Tom and Mac. Tom was younger and stronger. Mac was 10 or 11 years old with stiffness in his front legs. I was concerned he would play out, so I had to stop and rest him often.

We had to cross the bridge, climb the steep hill, traverse an open field, and look for an opening where the fence had been flattened. I had been guiding the team with the reins, but I couldn't see the trail. It was now nightfall with a fierce blizzard cutting visibility to 20 feet. The horses stopped suddenly; I checked and found a fence barring their way. I tied the team and followed the fence to find the opening, and in a few minutes, we were on our way. Tom and Mac plodded on and it was then I realized they were following the trail without my guidance. I simply slackened the reins and let them take over.

I was concerned how I could find our farm buildings, but it wasn't a problem. In this blinding snowstorm we reached home at last, safe and sound, thanks to Tom and Mac. My brothers took over their care and I went to the house to console my very worried mother.

When I found this story in Dad's papers after he died, it brought home to me, once more, our family's relationship with the valley and the bond Dad and Uncle Gerald had with it—the primary reason for their so-called experimental farm. The memory got me thinking back to when the government finished the Conestoga Dam in

1958, and how our valley playground had been flooded. By the mid-1960s, Dad and Uncle Gerald sold their farm for needed capital—the end of an era.

One summer's day about 50 years later, I walked from my brother Philip's cottage on the lake along the trail where we had played and where my father and our ancestors hiked and drove their horses. I entered into the conservation forest, now grown tall and dense on the slopes leading down to the water's edge. As I followed the trail deeper into the woods, I came to a small clearing containing a wild raspberry patch. I suddenly stopped, feeling a shiver down my spine, wondering if I might meet a bear. But all remained still, no rustling in the woods—only distant echoes of our youthful shouts of discovery on this land.

The abandoned buildings were gone but not the lessons we learned on this proving ground.

10

Girls, Hormones, and Bullies

From an early age, I thought a lot about girls as a means of diversion from the boring parts of being a boy, like school. Our classes were crowded due to the post-war baby boom—kids had started popping out all over town, out-pacing the number of school desks and rooms available. I attended Grade 2 in an overflow class in the basement of the Anglican church. At recess, we had to play in a small parking lot beside another yard full of clumps of black sandstone. We weren't supposed to play in it, but then why did they leave such a mess there? The stones provided a breakable material when we bashed pieces together. It hurt when we fell on this stuff while horsing around, and we had to explain our scrapes and bruises when we got home. But parents didn't complain in those days, leaving such issues to the judgment of teachers and school authorities.

ME WITH GIRLS, GIRLS, GIRLS IN GRADE 2

During recess one day in Grade 2, I proposed to a girl by the name of Mary Anne. I was bold enough to present her with a blue plastic ring, which I'd purchased for five cents at the Light & Life Bookstore and Gift Shop. She accepted and became my focus of infatuation. I daydreamed about her all the time. A couple of times she invited me to her place to play, but I swear I never showed her mine and she never showed me hers.

At the end of Grade 2, half the class was accelerated to Grade 4, but I was left behind in Grade 3, probably due to my daydreaming. A lot of the time, I focused on the back of girls' necks and hairlines—a big distraction for me.

Most of us attended John Mahood Public School, opened in 1954; a modern one-story affair with tall,

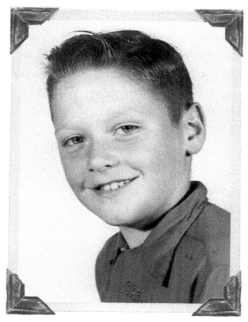

BEFORE I TURNED UGLY

north-facing windows, which only facilitated my continued distraction from schoolwork. There was no mid-
dle-school in Elmira, so our school's classes went from
kindergarten to Grade 8.

I passed every subject but didn't really apply myself, so
my report cards remained mediocre. I usually found the
lessons tedious and repetitive. I never learned to read or
write properly until much later. One of the few things I can
remember about those days is being made to stand at the
blackboard for not knowing something. I dreaded spell-
ing bees the most, especially when competing with smart
girls I would have liked to impress. I'd get all flustered and
make mistakes. I couldn't visualize words properly; had
to write them down, and that hasn't changed to this day.

One great diversion from all those contests was the school assemblies where they showed a cartoon movie with a "Duck and Cover" theme song that became popular throughout North America at the time. The cartoon involved a turtle taking cover inside its shell from a small stick of dynamite on the end of a string tied to a branch held by a monkey in a tree.

Of course, we had no personal shells to hide inside, and an atomic bomb would have blown up all of us and our whole school in a second. So, why did they show us this ridiculous cartoon and train us to dive under our desks? I guess it made some kids feel a little more secure. I didn't take any of it too seriously. But the exercise of diving down and clutching our heads with our hands, however futile, provided an exciting break from school work. At least it woke me up from my daydreaming for a while.

MONKEY BUSINESS AND THE ATOMIC BOMB

BEGINNING OF MY HORMONAL ONSLAUGHT

As I advanced through primary school, I tried to forget about girls for a while by focusing on other activities. What I lacked in mental advancement, I made up for on the physical side. My hormones soon went into 1st gear and I shot up in height. They called me "Big Neill." But my parents and teachers didn't tell me anything about what was happening to me. I recall it as a very mixed-up time because I didn't know what was going on inside my body. I remember thinking that I'd become pretty ugly and somewhat chubby. It was around the same time that I quit my Saturday cornet lessons and thought a lot about going to Dad's experimental farm on Saturdays, or going fishing and hunting—any possible means of escape.

I chummed around with Bruce Parker, a guy who took fishing and hunting very seriously. For a while, we spent many Saturdays together, tracking down rabbits in winter and trying to catch trout in country streams in spring. He learned all he knew on such matters from his father, an immigrant from Eastern Europe. Bruce told me his family name had been changed from something that sounded like "Perpupki." His father retained a heavy accent. When he sneezed, the air expelled from his nose and mouth with the forceful sound, "Russshhhiaaa!" We mused that perhaps with each sneeze he was reliving his escape from communist domination.

Besides Bruce, I sometimes hung around with some Mennonite boys. Elverne Bauman's parents belonged to a branch of Mennonites who were allowed to own black cars, whereas Peter Riest's parents were Old Order, so they drove a horse and buggy. These boys usually had to do the farm chores before school and they would sometimes arrive with manure on their boots. I remember being distracted by flies landing on the small pieces of dung, but I'd grown used to it by then. At times, I thought these guys were lucky. Children of farmers only had to be 14 years old to quit school, and some of them left on their 14th birthday. Our courses didn't include lessons on good farming practices, so why stay longer than you had to by law?

My friend Willard Martin lived on a farm on the western edge of town. His parents had a car and a truck painted in normal colors—new Mennonites. Willard started school late, like me, so he was also advanced, hormonally. Though he didn't have to stay in school, his family wanted him to complete Grade 8.

Willard didn't get along with Miss Wilfong, who taught us English grammar and literature. She was a single woman with gray hair held in a net. When she talked, her mouth seemed to be full of saliva, as if she needed to spit but couldn't during class. I actually liked her, but she had some funny ways. She would wait in the hall as we entered and usually began class by swinging the door shut as she repeated the verse of some prissy poem. For example, the opening stanza of John Keats' *Endymion*, which goes like this:

A thing of beauty is a joy for ever:
Its loveliness increases; it will never
Pass into nothingness; but still will keep
A bower quiet for us, and a sleep
Full of dreams, and health, and quiet breathing.

One day, Willard, Bruce, and I used binder twine to tie the inside door handle to the door handle of the closet behind. We made the twine just long enough so the door would abruptly stop before closing. The other students saw us setting it up and began to buzz in anticipation. Miss Wilfong entered while reciting one of her poems, but the hubbub made her so angry that she slammed the door hard. It bounced back and all the kids roared. She started to yank at the twine and the kids laughed louder. Miss Wilfong turned beet red. Willard, Bruce, and I, seated in the corner near the door, just grinned. She glowered at us and demanded the name of the culprit. No one spoke up. She probably blamed Willard more but marched the three of us to the principal's office.

Mr. Dunk, the principal, an elderly gentleman with a big red nose, had a hard leather strap with teeth. After a brief trial with a predetermined outcome, he lined us up and ordered us to hold out our hands. It really smarted, but I didn't cry or holler. Bruce was equally brave. Willard stood last in line. As the strap came whipping down, Willard pulled back his hand at the last second, throwing Mr. Dunk off balance. He rocked on his feet for an instant but didn't fall.

Mr. Dunk's face turned as red as his nose. I imagined him dying from a heart attack on the spot. After he recovered, he grabbed Willard's hands one-by-one and came down hard on them with his weapon. Then he began to shout at us, "You guys are the kind of idiots who would pay good money at a circus to buy a ticket to see a freak horse with its head where its tail should be. But when you enter, you're so dense you don't understand it's only a horse turned around in the stall."

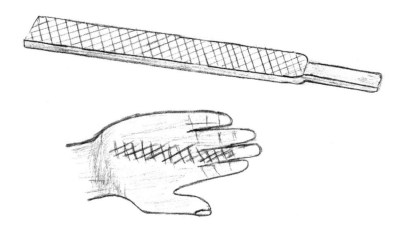

AN INSTRUMENT OF INSTANT "JUSTICE" AND THE EVIDENCE

He had repeated this dumb story so many times that it had lost its effect, if it ever had any. Besides, Willard lived on a farm, so he certainly knew where a horse's head and tail should be. I did too, after trying to be a cowboy on Dad's experimental farm. Mr. Dunk was clearly out of his league. Actually, I felt sorry for him because he had reached old age and didn't have any new stories to tell.

My growth spurt made me rambunctious and got me into worse trouble. One day at school, I came up behind a short guy by the name of Doug Brown in the boy's washroom while he stood peeing at the urinal. I liked him, but just horsing around I tugged the red-blue-green plaid scarf around his neck so hard that Brown started to turn blue. I panicked and grabbed at his scarf but couldn't get it off. My heart began to pound. Finally, I managed to get a finger under the knot and tugged it loose. Brown's face turned pink again. I apologized several times. He seemed a bit dazed and left in silent disgust, shaking his head.

I don't think he ever reported my near homicide, perhaps thinking that would cause me to bully him even more. But I had learned my lesson. By then I knew all about reform school. My first chance at reforming myself came shortly after this incident when the principal chose me and three other guys to be crossing guards. He issued credentials—badges mounted on white leather belts which crossed our chests. We took turns in the morning, at noon, and after school, assisting Dick Whittington, the old janitor from England and chief crossing guard at our school. Our job was to help little kids negotiate streetlights at the main intersection and at another pedestrian crossing down the road on the other side of the school. The duty had great benefits because, in addition to the belts and badges, we got to carry stop signs and could halt any cars—raw power!

One winter afternoon, when I had finished guard duty and was walking toward home, I saw this bully, Manfred, bashing Joe Foster's head into the ice on the sidewalk. With my newfound authority, I shouted at Manfred to cease and desist, "Let him go or I'll report you."

Such words had no effect on Manfred. He immediately rose and turned on me, fists flailing, while Foster ran home. We must have battled for an hour, slowly progressing down six blocks of Centre Street. He lunged at me relentlessly, but I dodged his blows or temporarily pulled him down. Finally, when he reached a point of total exhaustion, I pinned his face down in the snow and tightly held it there until he started to bawl. I let him go after he promised not to bash people's heads into the ice again. I watched him retreat down the street toward his house. That's the last time Manfred bothered little kids or me, my crossing guard authority firmly established. It felt good to stop a bully, and I learned to avoid bullying others for the rest of my life. [Much later I heard Manfred also straightened out—left town and became a successful businessman. In some small way, I hope I helped with his transformation.]

My larger size compared to other boys also gave me an advantage in extra-curricular activities such as Cub Scouts. I had been attending meetings on Wednesday evenings in our church basement for two or three years.

At the beginning of each meeting, we'd all stand in a circle, raise our three middle fingers in the air, and shout, "Akela! We'll do our best! Dyb, dyb, dyb—dob, dob, dob." I had no idea what "dyb" and "dob" meant and why it was included in the chant. Kids had to put up with a lot of unexplained nonsense in those days, and asking a lot of questions wasn't encouraged. [Searching for answers while writing this book, I learned we had been chanting short forms of "do your best" and "do our best" invented by Lord Baden Powell, who started the Boy Scout movement in Britain, in 1907.]

By 1957, I already had most of the badges I could earn for camping, cooking, hiking, swimming, and all that. I had been thinking of quitting Cub Scouts, but went to the first meeting in September anyway. That evening, the leaders named me "Senior Sixer"—the head cub in the pack—probably because of my size. I must admit, I didn't turn down the offer. The position gave me new status, power, and essential relief from boredom.

One Saturday in winter, we went day camping in the snow. That's when I learned, for sure, not to trust every adult's power and authority. I had to watch over each group of Sixes and see that they followed the orders of our cubmaster "Akela" and his right-hand man "Bagheera"—titles from animals in Rudyard Kipling's *Jungle Book*, not their real names (which I will keep secret). The troops had to build shelters and make campfires to cook hot dogs with pork and beans—basic survival skills.

By the early afternoon, I noticed Akela and Bagheera hadn't moved from their shelter and the campfire we had made for them in the morning. Akela kept saying,

"Neill, go out and make your rounds. See if anyone needs help."

I would come back in a half hour to give an honest report and they'd congratulate me. Bagheera would say something like, "Best check if they've all had enough to eat. We burn up a lot of energy in the cold."

As the day wore on, they became increasingly satisfied, even happy, with the progress of the troops I reported to them. Then I saw why. Our leaders had consumed a 26-ounce bottle of Canadian Club rye whiskey. By late afternoon, they just took my word on which groups of six should win the prizes for the best shelter and best campfire. As dusk approached, I arranged a quick award ceremony and we trudged back to the bus.

MOTTO: WE STAND OR FALL TOGETHER

By some miracle, they drove us home without incident or accident. I didn't report their drinking to anyone. They remained the final authority for Cub Scouts in our town and, anyway, no one would give you a badge for ratting on others—against the code!

When the school year ended, so did my term as Senior Sixer. In the fall, I went to my first meeting of Boy Scouts in the high school gym. All I remember is the older guys throwing hard drives at my head with basketballs—a kind of initiation? What was the benefit of getting your head bashed in by unsupervised sadistic jerks? That was the one and only meeting I attended. I figured Boy Scouts was another poorly-supervised club for hormonally-frustrated bullies who had no luck with girls.

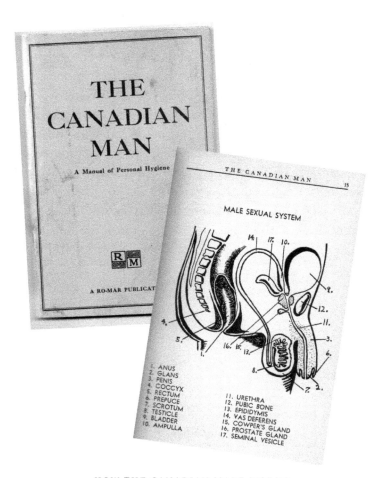

HOW THE CANADIAN MALE WORKS

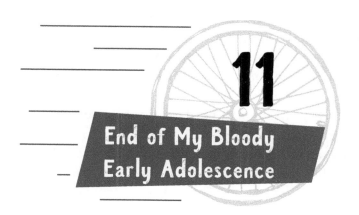

11

End of My Bloody Early Adolescence

I have to confess that I never forgot about girls, especially in Grades 6 through 8. I frequently masturbated while thinking about them at night—no wet dreams at all, as far as I can recall. My hormones were switching into 2nd gear. One day, Mom, finding stains on my sheets, left a small yellow booklet titled, *The Canadian Man: A Manual on Personal Hygiene*, on my bedside table, along with a box of tissues.

In this thin publication, I found interesting diagrams of male and female sexual anatomy, but the booklet provided no comparisons with the sexual organs of males or females from other countries and no explicit drawings of Canadian male and Canadian female organs coming together—a real cheat. The language was a bit too hard to understand, but I found some words claiming masturbation would not lead to insanity, as my friend Ted had told me. I read that too much masturbation might mean you had emotional problems, but, I thought: *What guy doesn't have that? Girls are pretty complicated and adults aren't much help.*

My parents found it hard to talk about sex. I learned a lot from other kids but didn't know if they really knew what they were talking about, like Ted on masturbation. I couldn't ask my friends questions because it would make me look dumb. The parts on female anatomy didn't really explain much about the purpose of girls' menstrual blood either, a thing which we joked about. It seemed like a really messy business to us.

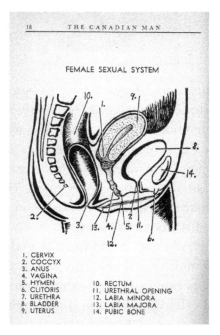

INSIDES OF THE CANADIAN FEMALE

138

The Canadian Man comprised the totality of my instruction on sex from adults until Grade 9, when we took "physical education." This consisted of various kinds of torture, like push-ups and jogging, as well as looking at more diagrams of sexual organs without clear explanations on sexual intercourse. But by then, I knew it all anyway, or at least thought I did.

Like most boys, I thought that becoming a sports star might give me an advantage with girls. I had become a good swimmer, and in the summers loved to frequent our outdoor municipal pool supervised by Pete Moss, who somehow managed to keep it free of algae. One time, I even managed to swim clear across Lake Conestoga and back.

In autumn, we played Canadian football, a rough and tumble game much like the American variety but a little faster since there are only three "downs," meaning each team only has three chances to gain ten yards, not four as in the U.S. I became pretty good at blocking and tackling, but not a great runner or quarterback. We wore shoulder pads and helmets without face guards, but it still was easy to get injured. Once when I tried to tackle a fast runner, he bashed me with his elbow, giving me a bloody nose. I quickly surmised it was a sport for "knuckleheads," as dad called them, who didn't care much about protecting their brains. So, I quit football.

I did a little better at softball. The coach put me on first base because of my height. I could reach pretty far to catch line drives and inaccurate throws by the rest of the team. I could also knock the ball pretty far when up

RESULTS OF PAUL'S WICKED SWING

to bat. But one time, while waiting for my turn, a guy by the name of Paul hit the ball and let go of the bat at the end of his swing. The thick end glided like a missile into my nose—yes, once again!—temporarily knocking me out. The other guys told me later that blood spurted out of my nose—like a geyser—and someone ran for help. The only good thing about this incident was that I finally understood why artists draw stars floating above someone who's been hit on the head.

When I got home, Mom filled a sock with ice and put it on my nose. Looking into the mirror in the evening, I worried I'd have to live with an enlarged snout. Would I end up looking like Mr. Dunk, our principal with the big red nose? After applications of ice, the swelling slowly subsided. Playing with Paul often led to such disasters. He slipped and fell down a lot, and usually wore broken and taped-up glasses. I don't know if he suffered from impaired vision or whether he was simply accident-prone—probably both. Anyway, I quit softball too.

I played street hockey with the guys, starting when I was about eight years old, using a tennis ball in warm weather and a puck after a snowfall, once the traffic had packed the road surfaces down. We shifted to the town arena as soon as hockey season started. This was my longest-lasting effort at team sports. It was serious stuff in our town because NHL stars had been produced by our senior local team, the Polar Kings. I started in Pee-Wee League and advanced to Bantam. My parents liked the fact I continued this sport, but I can only remember them coming to one game. Dad never helped with driving my team to play in other towns—too busy with his business. Mom had her housework, feeding all nine of us, including Grandma Neill, and many church and

BIG NEILL ON THE RIGHT BESIDE THE COACH
(THE SHRIMPS AT THE BACK ARE STANDING ON A BENCH.)

other social activities—not a "hockey mom," for sure. I kept my disappointment to myself.

In Bantam league, I did okay at playing defense because of my size. I could effectively block and check the smaller guys. But we didn't have helmets or face masks in those days, and in one game a driving puck hit me above my right eye. Blood spurted all over the ice. The assistant coach drove me to the doctor's office for seven stitches.

Actually, I never learned to skate very well; my left ankle always got tired and flopped over. So, I decided to quit hockey too. My parents didn't comment on this either—my decision. Probably it was because Dad never had the time or opportunity to play organized sports. After his father's early death, he was too busy with farm chores when he wasn't in school. When he first settled in Elmira, he helped to start a boxing club. He bought Glen and me boxing gloves one Christmas, but wisely never encouraged either of us to become serious boxers.

As I grew older, I developed the same philosophy as Dad. I didn't need clubs run by leaders who drank liquor on duty, or sports led by knuckleheads who would let bats knock you on the nose and pucks smash into your face. I resolved to stick with working at the factory after school. As far as team sports go, I figured three strikes and I'm out.

My regular work at McKee Brothers began with sweeping the floors after four every weekday. The job allowed Glen and me to earn good money. In the summer, we punched the clock like all the other laborers.

MCKEE HARVESTER AND HAY WAGON IN AN ELMIRA PARADE

We helped men cut, bend, and weld metal. Sometimes we worked on the assembly line. The products the factory made grew in number and Dad and Uncle Gerald employed more and more people from our town and the surrounding countryside. Almost everyone had heard about McKee agricultural equipment.

Glen and I learned a lot from skilled workmen—Canadians of Irish, Scottish, German stock, and recent immigrants from Poland, Hungary, Holland, and elsewhere. They knew we were sons of one of the owners, but we didn't ask for, nor did they give, special treatment—not that I was aware of, at least.

Working in the factory gave me new perspectives into the laborer's life. The work was tough and I could hardly wait for the buzzer to sound for breaks. A van would pull up in mid-mornings and mid-afternoons with refreshments, such as coffee or chocolate milk, long-john cream puffs, and meat pies. We could also take breaks to go to the toilet and buy those small glass bottles of Coca-Cola for about ten cents from the dispenser beside the punch clock. I would drink down four or five a day—a half-pound of sugar a week.

However, I had one big problem with this factory work. All the filth on my face and the Cokes I consumed combined with my 2nd gear hormones to create an ugly mess—blackheads and newly-emerging pimples. The powdered soap in the factory's washroom felt like sandpaper and stung my face. Before going to bed each night, I squirted these volcanic eruptions of puss and blood onto the bathroom mirror, washed my face with strong disinfectant soap, and, in the morning, I applied a layer of a plastic-like, skin-colored substance called "Clearasil"—the only disguise I had for meeting and talking to girls. I feared my hormonal overdrive would never end.

One summer, I worked on the assembly line, building large snowblowers, a new line of products for McKee Bothers. I injured my back while trying to lift a heavy metal part without bending my knees. After a visit to the chiropractor, the foreman put me in the stockroom. There, I gave out parts and materials to men and made them sign for company tools. I preferred this location in a quieter part of the shop, working under the tutelage of Johnny Wagner, where you could talk without shouting. My new job appeared to be a position of power, relatively speaking, but I tried to stay on equal footing with the men.

As each day proceeded, the faces of the men coming to the stockroom window grew more and more coated with grease and grime. Most wore dirty overalls, which they took home once a week to wash. I tried to understand the pattern of banter between them—their curses and sexist talk, especially when they caught sight of a secretary from the front office. They played practical jokes on other workers who had some weakness, strange behavior, or on so-called "pollocks"—their favorite ethnic target. I became so used to this behavior that it almost seemed normal, though I only observed and never jumped into the fray.

One time a worker taped a sign with the words "Ass Hole" to the backside of the foreman, a lanky guy who ran up and down the factory floor, usually darting this way and that with no apparent purpose, like a chicken with his head cut off. The joke brought attention to the fact he came from Owen Sound, which, if you look at a map of southern Ontario sideways, is at the exact location of an elephant's ass.

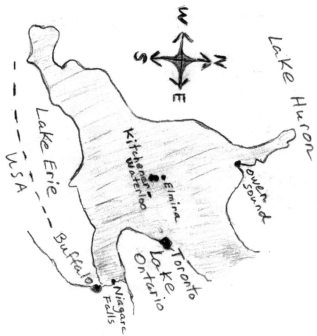

SOUTHERN ONTARIO VIEWED SIDEWAYS

One day, in front of some other men, the foreman said, "I'd better watch what I say because Neill might be my boss one day."

I replied, "No chance of that. I'd fire you right away." Later, I regretted my rebuttal because it had fed into his game, reinforcing a difference between me and the other men in our relationships. I preferred to be seen as just one of the gang.

Not all the workers joked and cursed. A few belonged to the Dutch Reformed Church—more subdued and religious immigrants. They didn't believe in organized labor. I remember them "ambushing" Dad at home one day during lunch break. They came to lobby him on preventing a union from forming at McKee Brothers. Dad agreed with them, but eventually United Steel Workers managed to sign up enough employees, and the pro-union side won. I don't think anyone ever called Dad or my uncle exploitive capitalists. They exercised fairness in pay and treatment of employees. They themselves had risen from difficult circumstances. I respected their position, but I could also see the workers' pro-union point of view.

Our parents purchased a wooded lot near the western edge of town, where they built a modern ranch-style house. It was located about a mile from the chemical factory, so those smells were not as strong. However, except for a woods to the east, we were in the middle of Mennonite farmers' fields, with the odor of fresh manure in the spring and fall. It took a few years before a suburb started to sprout up around us.

OUR NEW HOUSE ON FIRST STREET WEST

When the contractor finished the house in 1958, it was the "talk of the town." People must have thought we were rich, but Dad never took much money out of his business for his salary, so we never felt rich. I believe the main reason for building this new one-story house was to allow Grandma Neill to scoot around all the rooms in her wheelchair. By then her bad leg had given so much trouble that it had to be amputated. My parents also designed a family room with large windows, where she could sit through long winter days, forever crocheting, while watching the sun glisten on the snow and children playing in the nearby park. None of us kids could fault our parents for the move, for we all loved this old lady, born in Wisconsin in 1876.

I mention "fault" because the bedrooms were, in fact, smaller than those in our old house on Duke Street. My two brothers and I had to share one room and it became pretty smelly by morning, especially in winter when windows could only be opened a crack due to the cold. My sisters had to share a room too and my older sister Karen hated that. I recall a lot of crying, yelling, and telephone calls with her boyfriends and girlfriends. At the time, Pat Boone, Ricky Nelson, Brenda Lee, and Connie Francis had reached their zenith, and wearing what was seen in teen dances on television was a must. Mom took pity on Karen and assisted her in making a new dress, or altering an old one, for what seemed like every day of high school. Our new house also helped with her popularity for it had some great modern features, such as a built-in milkshake maker on the kitchen counter. Her friends thought that was cool, so sharing a room with her little sister eventually became less of an issue.

Dad preferred to do the finishing work and maintenance on our new property himself, a money-saving decision, probably, but he also loved to work with his hands. The year after we moved in, he started a rock patio at the back and a stone wall at the front. Glen and I helped him on Saturdays for some time—real tough work. If you weren't careful, you could easily crush your fingers between the heavy slabs and rocks.

One Saturday morning in early summer, Dad told Glen and me at breakfast that he expected us to work with him on the patio again. At the time, we were beginning to "feel our oats." I had reached my final height of five feet ten inches, towering four inches over Dad. Glen was about the same height. I had made other plans for the day and answered him sarcastically, "What do you think we are—Frankensteins?"

Dad, who almost never hit us, got so angry that he punched me in the face. The blow opened my old hockey wound and blood spurted onto the pancakes. I held back my tears. I could have taken him down in a bear hug, as I had done with Glen, but I could see him shaking a bit, so I sensed he probably had regrets for losing his temper. He had to drive me to the doctor's office for more stitches. When the doctor asked how it had happened, I just told him I'd hit my head, opening up my old hockey wound.

Although my head hurt a little, I worked on the patio for the rest of the day. I didn't need to apologize to Dad directly and I don't recall him saying sorry to me. We could see it in each other's eyes—a silent peace agreement, signed in blood. It took some years for my hormones to settle, but I never again shouted at him and he never again punched me—his authority accepted until I left home for good.

There are two events that marked the end of my bloody early adolescence: a trip to the USA and a death. In the summer of 1960, at the age of 14, I went with my parents and the twins, Philip and Frances, through Michigan and Illinois to Wisconsin, to visit our distant Haskins relatives in Green Bay. I knew they were my Grandma (Haskins) Neill's people, but not much else about them. They had some kids my age who wanted to know what it was like to live in Canada.

I said, "I just put away my dog sled and huskies for the summer before we came."

"No kidding! You're so lucky," they said.

GETTING THE GEOGRAPHY STRAIGHT!

I strung them along for a while like this, and they believed everything. Then I showed them Elmira on a map, located about one degree farther south than Green Bay. They gawked at the map, apparently ignorant about the location of any place besides their own city and state.

On the way home, we stopped in Chicago to see the new film, *Ben-Hur*. It's the story of Judah Ben-Hur, who is sold into slavery during Roman rule in Palestine. But he wins respect through his clever actions as a rower on a Roman galley in the Mediterranean and his skill as a chariot driver in the Colosseum. I loved this action adventure, especially how a bully called "Messala," with his golden helmet and black horses, gets paid back for his dirty tricks. Messala attempts to wreck Judah's chariot using the protruding spikes on his own chariot's wheels. As movie goers know, Messala tries to win by whipping his horses repeatedly, and then turns his whip on Judah. But finally, when Judah pulls the whip out of Messala's hands, Messala loses control and his chariot is destroyed. In a gruesome scene, he's dragged and trampled to death by horses and crushed under chariot wheels.

Did my seven-year-old twin brother and sister sit through all this blood and gore, including the crucifixion of Jesus? I can't remember. I do recall Mom crying a lot, even in the corny part when dark clouds gathered, the heavens opened, rain fell, and bloody water washed down from Calvary Hill, cleansing the world of sin, while washing the faces of Judah's mother and sister, curing them of leprosy.

At least seeing *Ben-Hur* in Chicago provided a diversion from the antics of my brother and sister in the back of our station wagon. I had grown increasingly annoyed with them and also with Dad's slow driving—his cautious rocking back and forth on the gas pedal and applying the brakes unnecessarily. When we reached home, as soon as we got out of the car I announced, "That was my last summer vacation with the family."

The second event happened at the end of summer, when I came home from somewhere—perhaps a weekend trip with a friend. Dad and Mom asked me to come to the kitchen table for a talk.

I asked, "What's it about? Did I do something wrong?"

Mom said, "No Neill, we just want to tell you that Peggy is dead."

This news shocked me. My little dog had grown old and fat, and I knew she wasn't particularly healthy. I'd largely ignored her in recent years. No one walked her.

I asked, "How'd she die?"

PEGGY, A FEW MONTHS BEFORE HER EXECUTION

Dad replied, "Very quickly and with no pain. I took her behind the shop and shot her. She never knew what happened."

I felt like crying but somehow held it in. I thought to myself, *How could Dad do this without asking me first?*

Mom said, "The dog was dying anyway—full of worms. Your dad just ended Peggy's misery."

This explanation didn't help much. Dad had buried Peggy on the spot, like a piece of garbage, whereas I would have liked to place her corpse in our garden and put a memorial stone above her, like I had seen kids do in the movies. Instead of expressing my anger, I stoically walked away to mourn in my room. It took me a long time to forgive my parents for not letting me participate in the decision and maybe the execution. (This happened a year before I killed two deer on the same day and gave up on guns for good.) For a while, I became fixated on the image of the bullet entering Peggy's skull and her brain exploding—blood shooting all around.

Then, gradually I came to understand Peggy's death as the end of my bloody early adolescence, and my 2nd gear hormones began to settle.

GLEN, KAREN, CATHARINE,
AND ME WITH THE SILVER BELT

Canadian Graffiti

As my hormones went from 2nd into a smoother 3rd gear, I began to follow my brother's and our friend Blake's lead. We often wore our shirt collars up and used lots of Brylcreem to curve our hair forward at the front and slicked down on the sides, forming a ducktail at the back, exactly like Elvis Presley. We had entered the Rock & Roll world of the early 1960s.

One time when my sexy first cousin Catharine came to visit from Vancouver with her protective mother, Aunt Ona, I became really infatuated with her, and she with me. We held hands in the back seat of our car and pulled back quickly whenever Ona took a sudden peak at what was going on. She appeared to be extremely suspicious and really gave me the evil eye.

Unlike Glen and Blake, I never wore a black leather jacket, a large back-pocket wallet with a chain, nor boots with noisy metal cleats on the heels, but I did wear a red and white leather sports jacket. Karen told our parents she really worried we were turning into "hard rocks." But Mom and Dad never said much—maybe not sure what Karen meant—and we didn't pay any attention to her.

This period of my life is embedded in my memory like a series of movie vignettes that appear to have little purpose until you reach the end. I kind of gave up the idea of escaping Elmira permanently, probably because of my gradually increasing mobility. This trend started in the summer after Grade 8 when I hung around with Eric, who already had a driver's license. My acne had started to recede and we spent time with a couple of girls whose fathers were educated professionals—kind of higher class. We did a bit of petting and necking but their parents guarded them fiercely, so they didn't have much freedom to spend time with us.

Eric borrowed his father's old sedan and once in a while his older brother lent him his new Chevy Impala convertible—a dreamboat. We'd cruise around town, trying to impress girls who liked to show off their figures by walking up and down Arthur, the main street in town. Sometimes we'd make our motor backfire for guys standing in front of Kerr's Restaurant, shouting comments and whistling.

Elmira's downtown area consisted of the one main street and a few side streets, but it had a lot of businesses to drive past besides Kerr's: Edgewood Restaurant, Bolander Shoes, Brubacher Shoes, Freiburger's Groceries, Otto's Men's Wear, W. C. Brown & Son's Cleaners and Tailors, Hendrick's Hardware, Weichel's Hardware, Hartman's Jewelry, Reichard's Dry Goods, the Light and Life Bookstore, Lishman Coach Lines, Central Cycle & Sports, Cale's Drugs, a music store, three banks, three gas stations, the post office, two barber shops and two real estate agents, the volunteer firehall, the Elmira Signet newspaper, the jail, and most finally, Dreisinger's Funeral Home.

We drove back and forth through town before stopping at Kerr's to shoot the breeze, play the jukebox, and drink a Coke or Pepsi. If we were hungry, we usually ate hot turkey sandwiches—white meat inside two slices of white bread, all smothered with milky gravy. Even the French fries were covered with the stuff and you had to eat fast or the food would get cold and too soggy.

Some Saturday nights, we drove to the nearby twin cities of Kitchener-Waterloo, blasting the hit parade from our car radio and trying to pick up girls. Once in a while, we would score by taking a couple of them for a ride to one of the A&W drive-in restaurants, where pony-tailed waitresses would come out on roller skates to flirt, take our orders, and then roll out again to serve us. We loved A&W root beer floats—large mugs of the sugary stuff loaded with vanilla ice cream.

This pattern of activity began to alter for me in January 1961 at an outdoor skating rink in St. Jacobs, a small village between Elmira and Waterloo, when I first really noticed Stephanie. She was tall with long brown hair and wore a flimsy, bright-red, Mexican-style jacket. She must have been freezing. I asked her if she would skate with me and she accepted, holding hands. As usual, organ music played as we went round and round. We talked easily and laughed a lot. I asked if I could see her again.

The following months became a challenge because I had to hitchhike in winter to her place. Her father, a truck driver, drank a lot of beer when off duty. He argued with Stephanie's mother, who seemed to be depressed all the time. Sometimes we hung out with Dicky, Stephanie's next-door neighbor. He had quit school, worked in a factory, and had a car. We went out on double dates together.

In the summer before I got my driver's license, I bought Dicky's old black 1947 Chevy Coupe for $100. [The Canadian dollar was worth slightly more than the U.S. dollar in those days.] I drove my car home and parked it beside Dad as he stood in our driveway. He said, "If it's yours, you'd better park it until you have your license." I promised I would.

I did, however, drive it down First Street to Dad's factory where, on weekends, I gave it a body job, grinding down and welding up all the holes and then applying Bondo, a putty that hardens like steel. For the next few months, this occupied a lot of my time and really burned up the money I earned working at Dad's factory. I took apart my Chevy's six-cylinder engine and gave it a ring and valve job to stop it from burning so much oil. At the factory, I spray painted it "virgin white with menstruation red rims," or so I told the guys, and coated the inside with a blue, fake fur upholstery called "Borg fabric," made in a nearby factory. Of course, my Chevy had to have white-rim tires too.

On my 16th birthday, I went for a driver's license test in Dad's humongous Mercury station wagon, a real tank with push-button automatic transmission control on the dashboard. I had been driving vehicles around the factory for years, so I felt confident during the test; so confident that I drove with only one hand on the steering wheel. The examiner failed me—an extreme disappointment because I had made plans to take off in the evening with Stephanie, finally alone in my car. I had to wait two weeks before trying the test again. This time I drove one of McKee Brothers' standard station wagons, using two hands on the wheel, and I passed easily.

Finally released from double dating, I could take Stephanie out with my souped-up Chevy. Drive-in cinemas provided a favorite venue. We never paid much attention to the storyline, which was too hard to follow because the speakers the cinema provided to hang on car windows produced low-quality sound. Normally, the sound of Stephanie and me, so passionately entwined, overpowered the soundtrack anyway.

STEPHANIE AND MY 1947 CHEVY COUPE

But the only result of all this was hickeys on her neck, a kind of trophy worn by some girls, which would fade in a day or two.

I was in love with that old '47 Chevy Coupe as much as I was with Stephanie. I installed a used car radio under the dashboard, held up by wires, and a long whip aerial with a raccoon's tail. On a clear winter's night, I could tune into an AM channel featuring a disc jockey we all loved. He called himself "Wolfman Jack." He broadcast from somewhere in the U.S., ranting and raving about anything that came into his crazy brain between playing the latest hits.

The flashiest car I ever bought was a 1953 Studebaker Sports Coupe—much ahead of its time. It had a powerful V-8 motor and it slumped low to the ground. I guessed it had been in an accident because it seemed to slink in and out of holes in the road, like a snake. I painted it cardinal red and polished up all the chrome,

ME WITH MY 1953 STUDEBAKER SPORTS COUPE

covering some of the rusty parts with silver paint. It only got about 15 miles (24 km) per gallon, so it really ripped a hole in my pocket. But what a great machine for drag races!

Some competition came from Old Order Mennonite guys who would leave home, driving a horse and buggy. They would park their rigs at a modern Mennonite friend's place, change their clothes, and take their hotrods out of storage. Then they'd speed those motorized beasts, usually painted black, with a whip aerial and lots of chrome. I especially recall one with many chrome stars. They'd peel rubber all along Arthur Street, looking for a challenger. We'd usually arrange to meet up on a straight stretch of Highway 86, the other side of the town cemeteries. I figured the restraint these Mennonite guys had to exhibit in their parents' homes throughout the week made them the wildest drivers on Saturday nights.

In those days, most of the older cars we could afford had standard transmissions with gear shifts on the steering column. Glen purchased a Foxcraft floor shift conversion kit and we learned how to copy it at the factory. He installed one in his car and he helped me mount one on my Studebaker's transmission. These devices attracted a lot of attention from the gang. Glen and I found ourselves doing a little side business, manufacturing and installing those floor shifts for other guys. It took us hours of greasy work to mount one of our counterfeits in place and we didn't charge a lot because our clients were friends. Besides, our copies felt a little loose and flimsy, and often our customers had to put up with motor fumes coming up through the floorboards.

We never fully mastered sealing up the holes we cut for installation, but our friends loved their new floor shifts—the definition of "cool."

Around the same time, I also advanced in two-wheel propulsion when I bought a 650cc Triumph motorcycle from a guy for about $75. He had taken it all apart and was either too lazy or too stupid to put it together again. I rebuilt the motor, replacing the piston rings and valves, as well as other worn parts. I worked for many months during the winter in my spare time. Finally, in spring, I finished the renovations by painting the frame red and black, with orange flames on the gas tank and wherever I could put them, to match its power. It could clock up to 90 miles (145 km) an hour, but it would start to shake when it reached about 80. I suspected, like my Studebaker, it had been in a crash.

Once I invited a group from our fledgling motorcycle gang to one of the abandoned farms rented by McKee Brothers on Lake Conestoga. This property included a

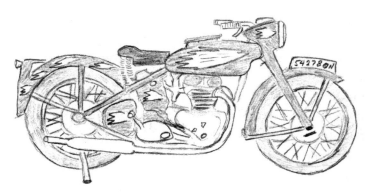

MY POWERFUL BUT SHAKY TRIUMPH 650

woods at the back, and Dad and Uncle Gerald had converted the house into a makeshift hunting camp. We invaded the place on a Saturday, with no intention of hunting. We cooked some food on the old cast iron stove and just horsed around. Some guys got drunk on the beer they brought and stripped naked.

After a few hours of this, someone spotted flashing lights down the hill at the gate. Some of the guys scrambled into the woods without their clothes, while others hid in the old barn. I looked down the hill and saw a black and white cruiser of the Ontario Provincial Police—we called them "the Holsteins." I got up my courage and went down to talk to them, explaining my father rented the land and I'd invited the other guys. Fortunately, they didn't have a warrant and couldn't investigate further.

We guessed a farmer's wife across the lake had spotted us and called the police. *She must have used binoculars*, I thought. A close call. After the Holsteins left, some of the guys mooned this distant busy-body with their mosquito-bitten asses.

That same summer, my friend Blake and I decided to attract lots of attention on our motorcycles by standing on the seats while driving down Arthur Street. Then we drove them along the railway tracks for about half a mile, exiting on another road.

The next day, the town's Chief of Police, whom we called "Captain Hook," arrived at our house. He asked to see my dad, who called me from my room. Hook made a couple of mistakes. First, he put all of his accusations into one mixed up charge—that I had been standing on my head on my motorcycle while driving on the railroad, or some nonsense like that.

I laughed and said, "Standing on my head? I'm not a circus clown!"

Hook found it hard to control his temper and I knew if I got him really angry, he would blow it. This strategy worked and he made his second mistake. He started to accuse me of hiding behind my dad's wealth. This made Dad angry because he never thought of himself or acted as if he were wealthy or privileged, and he taught us to do the same. He had risen out of poverty with only a primary education and his brains. He earned every penny he took home. They got into an argument and he ordered Hook to get out of our house.

I felt a little guilty for not admitting what I had actually done, but sensed some redemption when Dad took my side in the argument. He'd become one of the gang. That's when I finally forgave him for shooting my dog Peggy in the head.

All this concern with motorcycles, cars, and girls didn't do anything for my formal education. When I started high school, the authorities placed me in Grade 9A, which indicated they expected me to do well in the academic stream. In those days, "A" represented the top tier and if they placed you in "9E" or "9F," it meant they thought you were destined for a technical trade.

In 9A, I had to take Latin, although I didn't understand why. What was the use of a dead language, anyway? The Latin teacher, Mr. Eifert, a middle-aged man with a long Roman nose and balding head, had a slight low-German accent. The only thing I can recall about him is that he talked about blood a lot: "The Romans fought bloody battles with the Barbarian hordes.... Blood ran down the stones on the spot where they murdered Caesar.... Bloody chaos on the battlefield.... If you don't pay attention, blood will run down these aisles." I remember thinking, no wonder Latin is a dead language, everyone who once spoke it died a bloody death. At least his lessons kept me awake, but by the end of the year, I had my fill of his gory descriptions and threats, and I never took Latin again.

I continued to escape from such mind-numbing lessons by looking at girls' hairlines and necks (a habit formed in elementary school), and daydreaming about Stephanie. Elmira District Secondary School (EDSS) serviced all the outlying villages and farms, as it still does today, so Stephanie attended Grade 9 there as well. I would briefly meet her in the halls during class changes. She'd been placed in 9D or 9E, the commercial stream aimed at making students into secretaries and bank tellers. She didn't have to take Latin. I usually saw her fooling around with other "wild girls" as they walked down the halls. They all wore extra makeup and put their collars up. She often flirted with other guys, making me jealous, but I loved her free spirit and found her to be a lot of fun.

Our new house was only a few blocks from the school, so I walked there and back home for lunch, gulped down whatever Mom cooked, and then drove my car back to school, ready for the end of classes. Instead of joining extra-curricular activities such as sports or clubs for drama, singing, chess, curling, bowling, or the library society—activities I assumed were for brown nosers and pretentious overachievers—Stephanie and I would sit in my car after school or drive around to find a quiet place to neck a bit, until the school buses came to pick up out-of-town students. Then I would go to Dad's factory to sweep.

I must admit, however, that I did join the school band one year on the bongo drums and played a brief solo in *Granada* by the Mexican composer Agustin Lara. I had a pretty good sense of rhythm, but I still never learned to read music. Maybe I just wanted to make up for staring at Mr. Chislett's plastic nose so much, instead of paying attention during my Saturday lessons on the cornet.

I recall remaining quiet and obedient in French class because the teacher was really hot—short dark hair, shapely skirts and blouses, high heels, and intoxicating perfume. I dreamed about meeting her in Paris or some other exotic place. All our lessons included stories about France. Quebec didn't even exist because, according to our teacher, French Canadians couldn't speak proper French. [At the time, French had not yet become an official language of Canada, on equal footing with English. No one except French teachers and a few overachievers spoke French in Elmira. Montreal and Quebec City were far-away places—a different world.]

Ernie Kendall taught chemistry and biology, and I liked the lab classes, especially because we got to cut up frogs and look at their guts, causing some of the girls to squeal and the boys to laugh. In the spring, Mr. Kendall would take us on study tours through the nearby woods to see, among other things, Ontario's provincial flower, the great white trillium—a protected species. He was so serious about it. But a group of us boys would trail behind and fool around, not paying much attention.

Some would even sneak away to take a smoke break.

Once Mr. Kendall called me out in class, "McKee, you are just drifting down a river and you have no idea where you're going."

I added, "Correct, on a rubber raft." My smart-aleck remark earned me a detention. But I always knew how far I could push a teacher and never went beyond a certain limit. In detention period, I could actually get my homework done.

Mr. Kendall supervised "Teen Town," a wholesome opportunity for young people to get together and dance in the high school gym almost every Saturday night during the school year. Girls would sit on one side and boys on the other until a guy got up enough nerve to walk over and ask a girl for a dance. Of course, those who were "going steady," like Stephanie and me, would dance together all night. A guy would have to have a lot of balls to try to break in and ask a girl who was going steady for a dance.

Mr. Kendall carried around a six-inch ruler and stuck it between couples who, in his judgment, danced too closely together. That would cause some guys to take girls outside to the parking lot to neck, especially those girls who didn't care much about their reputations. Some also went out to smoke and drink. The only public place that served alcoholic beverages in town was the Steddick Hotel. But you had to be 21. This establishment had two entrances, one for "Gentlemen" and one for "Ladies and Escorts." I guess this strategy helped to keep out single women of ill-repute, but I never heard tell of any "frosty-prosties," as we called them, in our town.

We would arrange to get cigarettes and booze from an older guy whom we called "Waca." He spoke in a sophisticated manner. I knew he was smart because he could speak Latin pretty well. [You could only buy alcoholic drinks from the Liquor Control Board of Ontario or Brewers Retail, outlets which had been set up in 1927 after prohibition ended.] Waca was also underage, so I'm not sure how he managed. Maybe he impressed them with his Latin.

In the early days, we'd have him purchase sweet Mogen David wine, and later we graduated to beer and hard liquor. I only got thoroughly wasted a few times. Once, I participated in a vodka drinking contest and ended up puking up most of my stomach contents. I didn't make it home that night, telling my parents the next day my car had broken down and I stayed at a friend's place. They appeared to be oblivious to my various rebellious activities—still too busy with the twins, about age nine by then, and all of their own activities. That suited me fine.

I experimented with smoking for a while in my early teens, but soon learned cigarettes choked me up. I switched to Old Port Cigars because I liked their sweet wine flavor better, but they also made me clear my throat all the time, and they stank. I figured my parents would know I had been smoking, but they never brought up the subject with me. Neither of them smoked, but a lot of adults did in those days. Medical magazines in the doctor's office even contained cigarette ads. I tried a pipe for a couple of weeks. I liked the aroma of the dried tobacco; however, my taste buds became so badly burnt I couldn't tell one food from another—like shoving mashed-up cardboard down my throat. So, I quit smoking completely.

When I wasn't sweeping the factory or working on my car, I hung out with the guys at the pool hall on Saturday afternoons before going to pick up Stephanie. We'd shoot the shit as we played "spots and stripes" or snooker, on small-dollar bets. I'd have to breathe in their second-hand smoke, which also choked me up and made me clear my throat a lot. But that was the price I had to pay for being one of the gang.

I became so involved with Stephanie, my wayward friends, and my job at Dad's factory after school and Saturday mornings in order to earn money for fuel, car parts, and dating, that my grades slipped and they put me in Grade 10D and then 11C in the third year. A lot of guys dropped out, so they had to reduce the number of classes. I guess I hit the bottom. I didn't find school work difficult, simply boring as usual, so I never put much effort into it.

Because of my skill and knowledge, for my practical in Grade 11 auto mechanics Mr. Frey let me rebuild a Volkswagen car motor for Trevor Jarvis, the designer at Dad's factory. The other guys in my class only got to disassemble and assemble various parts. Mr. Frey was a modern Mennonite guy who spoke slowly and precisely, continually scrubbing his hands with a fresh cloth. He kept everything clean and in order. I respected him a lot and he treated me like the leader of the class. That's when I began to think about school in a different way. I knew Dad wanted me to go to university to study engineering and join his company someday. For a while, I gave up all thoughts of leaving Elmira and assumed that's what I would do, though I didn't apply myself in mathematics and science—plenty of time for that later, or so I thought.

On one occasion, I brought Stephanie home for a Sunday dinner with the family. We normally held proper Sunday evening meals at our house in our separate dining room, with Dad's Mantovani records playing in the background. Dad would carve the chicken or roast beef in front of us, give out small portions, and pass the plates around. We had to remain at the table for dessert and conversation—no dashing away. I think our home and family both impressed and intimidated Stephanie. She mainly experienced arguments and conflict in her own home, especially when her dad got drunk. We talked about it when I drove her home and she cried.

Bringing home Stephanie, the girl I spent so much time with after school, on the phone, and on weekend dates, led my dad to pronounce the next day, "Just keep your pecker in your pants." Dad had suspected we might be going too far. Actually, I considered this one sentence to be an influential piece of advice. He never said as much, but I knew if I got her pregnant, I might end up being a tradesman with a young family and would never make it to university and become an engineer.

Although I avoided becoming a teenage father, I did get into a different kind of trouble with Stephanie. During the last period of our relationship, we spent time with her older brother Barry, who had recently been released from reform school. I think he'd been locked up for theft. She wanted to keep him on the straight and narrow and asked for my help.

Barry was a loose cannon. He talked too loud and drove too fast. One time, he was driving us in their father's car on a gravel road when he hit the soft shoulder and lost control. The car flipped upside down in the ditch. When it came to a rest, I remember all three of us lying on the roof, looking out the back window. We laughed nervously and then Barry started to cry. He yelled in agony that his father would never forgive him. Stephanie demonstrated tenderness and reassured her brother all would be okay. We had to walk back to the highway and flag down help to order a tow truck. But the car was a total wreck.

I understood Barry to be quite a tortured guy and I took pity on him. He got a job and tried to reform. One Saturday in winter, I helped him fix an old car he had bought, using the facilities at Dad's factory. I had forgotten my keys, but we easily entered through a back window, which was never locked. Barry and a friend returned one night a few weeks later—went in through the same window and broke into the office. They stole the safe, which had little of value in it, and headed into the countryside with their loot, laughing and drinking a case of beer. The police stopped them and found them drinking while driving, and soon discovered the safe in the trunk. Real bright!

Barry went to prison this time, not reform school. The incident more or less ended my "steady" relationship with Stephanie. By then, she had quit school to work in a factory so she could afford nice clothes, makeup, and the latest LPs. I dated her a few times after that and met her at a dance in early 1964, when she told me she was pregnant and would soon marry the father. That ended any element of my former fixation on her.

By then I had started to date other girls from outlying towns, even one from Toronto. I sold my old Studebaker and bought a two-tone green 1956 Mercury. Its crown gear whined loudly at high speed—something I couldn't afford to fix. During winter, I joined my friends in racing down side roads, sliding and twirling our cars on the ice and snow. The object was to make a 360 degree turn without rolling over. I became pretty good at it.

During that period, I spent more time with our gang: Wally, Eddy, Lyle, Fred, Bruce, Brian, Fishy, Blake, and for a while, Glen. Some of them were Catholic and lived northwest of town in "Catholic country," not far from the McKee home farm. We attended dances in Catholic church basements on Saturday nights. The gang held stereotypes about girls; for instance, Catholic chicks were sexier, compared to stuck-up Protestant girls. We could get wine and beer in their area because more people drank in Catholic country—a normal thing to do. Some of the guys' parents even made their own wine in their basements. The priests drank real wine at Catholic masses—no Welch's Grape Juice. A lot of our jokes were about the priests and their drinking habits.

Historically, most Protestants and Catholics lived in separate areas of the countryside around Elmira. But my father employed a Catholic woman, Marina, as his secretary, and two other Catholics: Jim, as foreman, and Frank, as purchasing agent. Dad tried hard not to carry on the prejudices he'd grown up with and I respected him for that. He said his mother was quite bigoted, in spite of a story he told us—how their Catholic neighbors had been the first to show up to help the McKee family when his father was killed on the farm in 1933.

By this time in my young life, I was becoming more aware of prejudice and conflict. I had "graduated" to cleaning the company office after school. This allowed me to witness something that made me uneasy about my future plans. A few times I saw Dad and Uncle Gerald argue about business deals. They'd sometimes even get into shouting matches. I remembered how some of their other brothers, who had been involved in the business, likewise got into disagreements with them. One by one they had dropped out, for various reasons. Dad told me on more than one occasion, "Business and family don't mix." This pronouncement stuck firmly in my head.

On occasional weekends in summer, some of our gang would drive north to Wasaga Beach on Georgian Bay—a fantastic strip of golden sand and cool water with lots of midway amusements: junk food, pinball arcades, and rides. We'd cruise up and down the beach to try to pick up girls. We did a little boozing, but carefully avoided drinking while driving and possibly getting stopped by the police, because it could mean losing your driver's license and being hopelessly grounded.

We usually took the grooviest car owned by one of the guys who had quit school and was earning good money. Fred's 1955 Chevy Bel Air Sports Coupe was my favorite, but he drank a lot, so quite often I became the designated driver. One night when heading home on Highway 400, the major north-south artery of southern

LETTING THE GIANT CROSS THE HIGHWAY

Ontario, I saw something ahead of us and came to a halt in the middle of the highway.

"What the hell! Why did you stop here?" Brian asked.

"To let the giant cross," I said.

They hooted and that woke me up enough to drive again. I hadn't been drinking but really did think I'd seen a giant crossing the road. I must have been exhausted from our weekend's antics.

After one of these trips, when I was cruising around on a Saturday afternoon, I really did see something both real and tragic—not a dream at all. While heading south out of town on Highway 85, I passed a small brick house. I could see police cars and policemen in the driveway, as well as two white sheets spread out on the lawn. I slowed down to take a good look but never learned the full story until the next day. Two brothers, who drank a lot and used to bully me and my friends, had been fighting over the same girl. One of them took a shotgun and killed the other and then turned it on himself. I considered the incident a wake-up call on heavy drinking and the emotions of youth. I never thought something like this could happen in our peaceful little town.

My friends and I talked about driving down to Buffalo because, in those days, you only had to be 18 years old to drink alcohol in New York State. We also talked about meeting sexy black girls—another stereotype that infused our juvenile minds. I can't recall ever making it there—it was only guy talk. Such images from American culture, which seemed more tantalizing than the familiar, penetrated Ontario.

A decade later, when I saw the movie, *American Graffiti*, I realized how similar my early years of high school had been. In the movie there's a guy called "Toad." In Elmira, we called him "Fishy." He looked and acted the same—kind of clumsy and disheveled in appearance, with a brush cut, pimples, and heavy-rimmed glasses which always fell down his nose. Fishy often played the role of joker, as did Toad, who, in the movie picks up a wild blonde on the street while driving around in his friend Steve's convertible.

In the movie, set in Modesto, California, Steve and Laurie are going steady. He intends to join his friend Curt and fly off to college the next day. Steve is much in love with Laurie, and he vows never to leave her. He promises to return and marry her someday.

Physically, the character I identified with is John, who combs his hair forward at the front and into a ducktail at the back, held in place by Brylcreem—like me and others in our gang. John cruises the streets in his hotrod all evening, looking for a drag race challenger. (Actually, I never took up drag racing seriously. It burned up too much fuel, ruined your tires, and required too many repairs. Nevertheless, I identified with what I saw on the screen.)

In the movie, friends meet up at a drive-in restaurant where they are served by pony-tailed girls on roller skates, a scene familiar to us. We also had similar confrontations with the police, though not so exaggerated as in the movie, when the guys manage to rip off the back axle of a police car.

In Elmira, we listened to the same screeching voice of Wolfman Jack and the same hit parade played in the soundtrack of our lives—*One, two, three o'clock, four o'clock, rock; Why do fools fall in love?; At the hop; You're 16, you're beautiful, and you're mine.* When I saw Steve dancing with Laurie to *Smoke gets in my eyes*, it reminded me of how I used to dance close to Stephanie at Teen Town.

As the movie plot progressed, my attention shifted to Curt, played by Richard Dreyfus, the narrator of the story. Curt is supposed to leave for college the next day, but he appears to be getting cold feet. Then he meets Wolfman Jack in a surrealistic and rather disappointing way. It's evident Wolfman is kind of a fake and a letdown, but, surprisingly he tells Curt not to waste his future—to get on with his education.

In the morning, it's Curt who flies off on a plane for university, leaving Steve, Laurie, Toad, and John behind to live out their lives in their hometown. When the end titles come up, we learn Steve marries Laurie, never goes to college, and becomes an insurance agent in town. John stays put with his cars and women, whereas Toad loses the draft lottery and is killed in Vietnam. Curt finishes university but then flees to Canada as a draft dodger and becomes a writer.

The movie script compresses all that happened to our gang and me into a single weekend, whereas, in reality, such storylines take time to mature. I still had one and a half years of playing Curt to go. Like Curt, I would finish university and eventually become a writer, and like him, my rebellion against the norms of strait-laced, do-gooder, North American youth culture, gave me lessons and insights I would never forget.

MY WORLVIEW WAS KNOCKED IN A NEW DIRECTION

13
Travels with Holden Caulfield

On Friday November 22, 1963, our principal, Mr. H. B. Disbrowe, called an assembly of the whole student body to tell us President Kennedy had been assassinated in Dallas. I felt numb. It was the kind of shock that knocks your worldview in a new direction, although you don't really know it at the time. By then I'd started to read the newspaper and watch TV news. Like many Canadians, I had been fascinated by John Kennedy and his glamorous wife, Jackie. His standing up to the Soviets during the Cuban missile crisis the year before had really impressed me. I'd only made that one trip to Wisconsin and wanted to see more of America.

Jumping forward to the end of the school year in the summer of 1964, I worked at McKee Brothers, as usual, but took off on a vacation trip to the U.S. for about 10 days with a friend by the name of Bruce in his MG sports car. By then I had phased out of hanging around with the usual gang, but I enjoyed Bruce's ironic sense of humor. I was itching to get away from the familiar places of Ontario for a different kind of vacation, and Bruce was the only friend I knew with an interest in going elsewhere.

And so, we headed to New York City and the World's Fair, where we rode on the cable cars called the "Swiss Sky Ride" and a giant tire-shaped Ferris wheel, took a monorail gliding through the amusement area, watched helicopters flying all around, and admired the steel globe in the middle of the so-called "Fountain of the Continents." We entered the International Area—a global village. For the first time I saw live Polynesian dancers, a Thai pagoda with Buddhist monks, and a Mariachi band from Mexico. I heard the gongs of Indonesia and the drums of Ghana. My childhood fantasies about "Africa," on the far hill the other side of the chemical factory, rushed back into my mind.

Over 100 restaurants on the grounds offered food from all around the world. I wanted to stay and take it all in, but Bruce found the crowds overwhelming. Besides, this fair had no proper midway and the temperature soared in the middle of the day.

Bruce and I found New York City itself dirty and unfriendly. The skyscrapers seemed to close in on us, as drivers honked their horns and shouted when Bruce hesitated just a little. But the sexy women on the streets were something else! Lucky for me, I wasn't driving.

I had read in the New York Times that riots in Harlem had recently ended. A 15-year-old by the name of James Powell had been shot and killed by a white off-duty policeman. Harlem's black community rose up in

TWO ELMIRA HICKS IN NEW YORK

anger, looting and burning. We stayed clear of that part of the city.

On the journey, I had started reading *The Catcher in the Rye* by J. D. Salinger. I think it had been recommended by my English teacher, Mr. Exley. It certainly wasn't on the curriculum. The main character in the novel, Holden Caulfield, is around the same age I was at the time. He's from a rich family who put him in a prep school to try to reform him, but he's expelled for failing most of his subjects. He gets into arguments with his friends and comes to hate everyone—finds them to be "phonies"—and escapes to New York City. There he explores the seedier side of life: dirty hotels and bars, prostitutes and pimps. But he finds their world phony too. He says, "I was surrounded by phonies.... They

HOLDEN CAULFIELD

were coming in the goddam window." I identified with Holden's longing for authenticity since I'd gone through similar feelings in high school, and I started to see New York and America through his eyes.

From New York, Bruce and I headed to Washington, D.C., and Arlington, Virginia, where we visited the gravesite of President Kennedy. I fell silent as I stared into the eternal flame, thinking, what a stupid waste. What ridiculous country could kill off its dynamic young leader? I saw some people placing flowers by Kennedy's memorial. This seemed useless too, for as Holden says, "Who wants flowers when you're dead? Nobody."

After the cemetery, we drove through Washington and somehow found ourselves, two white boys from Canada in a red sports car, caught in a poor black neighborhood. What a great target we made! We quickly got back on the highway and headed through the small towns of Virginia and up into the mountains, taking the Blue Ridge Parkway into the deep South. We stayed in cheap motels a couple of nights on our way to Miami to swim in the ocean. I wanted to stay a while to take in all the beautiful women tanning on the beach—maybe even meet some like Holden did. I loved this carefree lifestyle. But Bruce wanted to move on. By then, I knew he would never stop in one spot very long.

We drove farther south through the Everglades, looking at shacks owned by poor people—probably blacks and Seminole Indians—some with Cadillacs parked out front. When we reached the end of the road, we took off our shoes and stepped into the warm water of the Gulf of Mexico. We stayed overnight in some junky joint, and at breakfast the next morning, Bruce suddenly announced we were going home. I wanted to take in more sights and eat more fresh seafood, but it was his car so he called the shots. I'd been studying Bruce and decided he and Holden Caulfield had a lot in common—mainly being negative about so many things. Fortunately, his witty sense of humor compensated for that, and we laughed at the same things.

In the novel, Holden searches for something more authentic but doesn't know how to find it. He decides to go out West, but in the end doesn't do so. Instead, he gives into his family's wishes and undergoes psychiatric treatment for his aberrant behavior. To me, he seemed to be a normal rebellious adolescent. It takes one to know one, and I'd already gone through all that.

We reached Elmira after about 70 hours, only stopping for gas, washrooms, food, and short sleeps. Bruce had done most of the driving. He was exhausted but really happy to be home. I felt kind of let down—back in this too familiar place so soon. Our wandering had been quite aimless but enticing for me, and it solidified my thinking about needing a completely new direction in my life, a journey which I had already started.

By the end of the trip, I had finished *The Catcher in the Rye* and said goodbye to Holden for good.

14

The Times They Are A-Changin'

Going back a few months before that trip to the U.S., I can recall the chill and darkness of one rainy Sunday evening in March 1964. I had finally and completely broken with Stephanie and was driving around, directionless, in my latest car—a black 1955 Pontiac hardtop. As I rounded the corner on First and Arthur streets, I noticed the lights were on in our United Church—a modern building erected in the late 1950s. On a whim, I pulled into the parking lot, walked in, heard voices coming from the basement, went downstairs, and entered an ongoing Young People's meeting. The group attracted youth from a cross-section of Protestant denominations.

When I entered the room, I heard some of the girls gasp. Since Grade 8, I had paid little attention to these people I considered "goody-goodies." In turn, I think many of them had written me off as a lost cause. But they didn't demonstrate any hint of such bias during the evening. They welcomed me and involved me in the ongoing discussion. Possibly due to my different experiences and points of view, I drew a lot of attention. When I returned for the next meeting, the group was in the process of voting for a new vice president because the guy in that position had resigned. To my surprise, someone nominated me, I accepted, and was elected.

A university student by the name of Bob Kavanagh supervised the group. He took an immediate interest in me. At the time, Bob was planning to become a United Church minister. As the weeks went by, he introduced me to modern theological books, such as Paul Tillich's *The Eternal Now*, Dietrich Bonhoeffer's *Letters from Prison* and Martin Buber's *I and Thou*. Bob preferred questions rather than answers to stimulate deep discussions. I'd never experienced this approach before. I had almost phased out of attending services at our church—only at Christmas and Easter to please Mom.

Bob led me to get to know our new minister, Reverend Alvin Evans. I learned that a decade earlier, he'd been an officer in the Royal Canadian Mounted Police. As he told it, one day while pursuing a criminal across the plains of Saskatchewan, he stopped his police car, turned around, and drove to his headquarters to resign. He'd had an existential crisis out West and knew he had to find something more meaningful to do with his life. He returned to Ontario to complete a theology degree and become an ordained United Church minister.

Al, as we called him, loved to discuss any issue, including my doubts about taking the Bible literally. He delivered somewhat cerebral sermons, which were a little hard for a lot of the congregation to digest. Many would have preferred him to harp on Bible stories and ideas within their comfort zone. Eventually, I concluded Al really didn't belong in our town—too liberal for most people. Before coming to Elmira, he and his wife had spent a year in the East End of London, England, ministering to poor parishioners—a real contrast to middle-class Elmira. He had also nearly completed a Ph.D. in clinical psychology and had a part-time job as a student counselor at the University of Waterloo—one of the conditions he had made before accepting the post in Elmira.

For the rest of Grade 12, I helped run entertaining events at Young People's meetings, made new friends in school, and sparked new conversations. But my main focus had to be on catching up for lost time in my studies. Ontario, at the time, had five years of secondary school and I knew the culminating curriculum of Grade 13 would be tough. It involved passing province-wide, do-or-die, government exams.

In September of 1964, after returning from that trip to the U.S. with Bruce and Holden, the Young People's group elected me president. We added religious discussions on faith and doubt, skits, folk music, and dances. Our membership grew rapidly. My mom thought I might become a United Church minister, after all. But by then I had started declaring that I was an agnostic. Through discussions with Bob, I found myself more interested in other religions and philosophies, such as

ON MY WAY TO ZEN WITHOUT THE ELVIS HAIRCUT

Zen Buddhism, and read about it in Alan Watts' book, *The Way of Zen*. I began to float in spiritual and intellectual dreams. So much for my mother's hopes!

Due to the pressure of my studies, the Young People's group remained the only extra-curricular activity I could afford to include, besides spending time with Ruth Howey. She lived on the next block and was a year behind me in school. Her family attended our church and I can remember her seated in a pew, wearing white gloves. To me, she seemed all prim and proper, until I got to know her. I doubt if Ruth was one of the girls to gasp at my dramatic entrance into that Young People's meeting.

Through discussions with her and our talks with Bob, we began to experience many new realms of thought together. Ruth was frank, expressive, and self-critical. I had too much confidence, at least on the surface, and she made me think about things. We analyzed ourselves and other people, becoming close, emotionally. When we talked, sometimes I felt I could read her mind, and she could read mine. We could pick up any conversation exactly where we left off. Our relationship became more than platonic, but we carefully limited ourselves to kissing and necking.

Rev. Al and his wife Barb, as well as Bob, were good friends with the Panagapkas, a Ukrainian-Polish family of two brothers and their wives and kids. They lived together in a farmhouse on the outskirts of town. I had seen this house from our kitchen window across the fields, but had no idea such people lived there. Their home was always open for conversation and laughter—a pot of coffee ready on the stove. At the time, Ed Panagapka, the older brother, held the position of production manager at Dad's factory, where he spent up to 14 hours a day, perfecting systems and talking over issues with employees and friends. When he came home, he would join in the conversation on any subject. His wife, Toni, would offer wise and succinct comment from a more emotionally mature perspective, often correcting her husband in an affectionate way.

Wally and Jeanette Panagapka were struggling with new teaching careers, while Toni looked after their child, along with her and Ed's growing brood, who I would occasionally babysit while studying. I loved to play with little kids and regretted I'd ignored my two younger siblings, Philip and Frances, during my rebellious years.

I could feel my brain expanding by the day while I learned to participate as an equal. The Panagapkas respected my opinions, and Ruth felt the same. Neither

PANAGAPKA KIDS, A FEW YEARS LATER

of us had experienced such discussions with older married people before. Ruth's parents usually treated her like a child and my parents considered such discussions, analyzing everything, a waste of time.

During one discussion at the Panagapkas, Ruth imitated a Zen Buddhist monk and gave me a slap on the face without warning—to awaken my consciousness. Then we rolled on the floor, laughing. The Panagapkas probably wondered what was going on since they were not familiar with Zen.

In Grade 13, I also started to really connect with my teachers on an intellectual level for the first time. I especially remember Bob Huschka, a teacher who had lived through World War II in Sudetenland, a German-speaking part of Czechoslovakia, which was annexed by Germany in 1938. Mr. Huschka had escaped war-torn Europe with his parents in 1947, when he was 13. His first language was Czech and his second German, but he spoke English clearly, pronouncing every sylla-ble with no definable accent. When he taught us about the war, I detected an occasional tremor in his voice as he described the goose-stepping Nazis advancing through Europe, and their murder of six million Jews in the Holocaust. He even became teary-eyed when speaking sometimes, probably thinking about the boy-hood home he had fled. I knew he had had experiences he would never tell us about directly. His emotional delivery increased my interest in history and politics and I began to think that political science might be an option for me.

I became more interested in English literature than ever before, largely because of the way our teacher, Bill Exley, taught. He was only about five years my senior, and he connected well with many students. At the end of our study of Robert Bolt's play, *A Man for All Seasons*, on the life and death of Sir Thomas More, Chancellor of England during the 16th century, Mr. Exley wore cleri-cal robes and played organ music on a record player. He dramatized how More refused to endorse King Henry VIII's divorce from Catherine of Aragon, when she proved unable to provide him with a son. Thomas More objected to the divorce on moral and religious grounds because he was a strong Catholic in a country then dominated by the Roman Catholic Church. His stand against the King eventually cost him his head.

Mr. Exley raised such moral questions and taught literature in an unconventional way. The play deeply moved me, but some of the guys in my class made fun of Mr. Exley's eccentricities; for instance, he required everything to be in order before he started class, including equal spaces between each piece of chalk on the ledge of his blackboard. As he greeted students in the hall, a couple of guys would walk in and slide all the chalk to one end. When Mr. Exley entered, he would angrily put each piece back in place, then try to calm his nerves before starting the lesson.

I'd already tortured teachers enough at that point in my life, so I didn't partake in these juvenile antics. I had more interest in reading and discussing history, philosophy, and literature, including the short stories—fiction, creative nonfiction, and essays—in *Man and his world*. The book contains the works of famous Canadian, American, and international authors such as William Faulkner, Stephen Leacock, Robert Davies, Bertrand Russell, C. S. Lewis, Somerset Maugham, and James Joyce. We studied an essay titled *East and West*, by Rabindranath Tagore (1861-1941) from Bengal, India, which took me further on a path away from the engineering and science of the West toward the spiritual and philosophical answers of the East. This shift took place gradually, not in any sudden revelation. I loved Tagore's words:

The wriggling tentacles of cold-blooded utilitarianism, with which the West has grasped all the easily yielding succulent portions of the East, are causing pain and indignation throughout the Eastern countries. The West comes to us, not with the imagination and sympathy that create and unite, but with the shock of passion—passion for power and wealth. This passion is a mere force, which has in it the principle of separation, of conflict....The world today is offered to the West. She will destroy it, if she does not use it for a great creation of man. The materials for such a creation are in the hands of science; but the creative genius is in Man's spiritual ideal.

These new ideas danced in my head for the first time as I discussed them with some of my more mature Grade 13 classmates, including Ken Frey, who came from a Mennonite background and had an interest in philosophy and religion—interests which made him a friend for life.

RABINDRANATH TAGORE

Mr. Exley spent many hours commenting on and correcting my pompous prose and pretentious poetry with a fine red pen. He also lent me his copy of the LP, *The Times They Are A-Changin'* by Bob Dylan. My mind stretched wide open as I listened to Dylan's lyrics for the first time. New images and ideas came rushing in about my present world and future choices. Nothing seemed impossible.

In contrast, in Mrs. O'Grady's French classes we studied *La Petite Poule D'Eau* (The Little Red Water Hen), by Gabrielle Roy, a story about a large French-Canadian Catholic family in rural Manitoba—*Finally, a Canadian theme in French class,* I thought. But the story, part of the all-Ontario curriculum, portrayed French Canadians in a patronizing manner, reinforcing stereotypes. Once again, our teacher never facilitated discussions on Quebec, a no-no political topic. By 1964-65, the Front de libération du Québec (FLQ), a separatist and Marxist-Leninist paramilitary group, was planting bombs—a "not so quiet revolution" against domination by the Catholic Church and conservative provincial forces that helped to keep French Canadians in their place, reinforcing the *status quo*, including economic and political domination by English Canada.

Al Evans allowed me to study in a church meeting room to escape the noise of my young siblings at home. I worked like a monk in a cloister. One of my classmates, Bill Scarrow, joined and helped me with math, at which he excelled. At the beginning of Grade 13, I had opted for both trigonometry and algebra because I still hadn't decided what I would study in university. I could handle trig because it was less abstract, but I struggled with algebra.

Fortunately, I had a great teacher, Mrs. Denholm. She exhibited patience and wisdom, nurturing me through the year. She also happened to be the sister of John Kenneth Galbraith. In fact, she looked like a female version of that famous Canadian-born economist, civil servant, author, teacher, and diplomat, who advised President Kennedy and others, trying to make America more liberal, with a planned economy. [As it turned out, Mrs. Denholm had greater success with me and my algebra studies than her brother ever had in his reformation of America, but he did write a lot of important books, which influenced the policies of many countries, including Canada.]

When I finally faced the province-wide Grade 13 algebra exam, I sat there trying to complete each problem, only coming to dead ends. After two hours, our time was up and I walked out thinking I had failed. Then I learned from the other students and Mrs. Denholm herself that the exam was unduly tough. Surprisingly, the English literature exam was also very difficult—*Maybe created by nerds*, I thought. Some of the smartest students felt the same. I could only cross my fingers.

I did better at physics and chemistry. But I still equated chemistry with the continuing stinks we had to endure in our town, though not as bad at our new house on the west side, as previously mentioned. By the 1960s, the chemical factory had new owners who renamed it "Uniroyal Limited." [Many years later, I found out that, at the time, Uniroyal was one of seven North American facilities busily making Agent Orange for America's Vietnam War. Agent Orange was composed of two herbicides, 2,4-D and 2,4,5-T, which Elmira's factory had much practice and expertise in manufacturing, beginning in the 1940s. The Americans wanted to destroy the enemy's crops and the jungle that concealed Vietcong and North Vietnamese troop movements and supply lines. U.S. Armed Forces dropped about 21 million gallons (80 million liters) of this chemical concoction on Indochina. The formula, produced at many times the potency needed to kill vegetation, had disastrous effects throughout the decades that followed. Thousands of Vietnamese, Cambodians, and Laotians died of cancer and suffered from other diseases. In addition, thousands of fetuses were aborted or maimed with birth defects, leading to disabilities. Uniroyal was doing America's bidding, while the company increased Elmira's tax revenue and paid for many salaries of townspeople. See more details in the *Postscript: Closing the Circle*.]

During 1964-65, I, like most fellow students, teachers, and town residents had no clue Elmira would become such an infamous player on the world stage. Most people remained pretty much out of the loop on the Vietnam War as well, because big demonstrations against it had not yet begun, at least in Canada. There were a few rumors about cattle dying from drinking the water in Canagagigue Creek, but few people became alarmed about this. I can still picture the creek's spooky beasts, which I had seen as a kid, but I never returned to that ghostly place to investigate.

In the last week of classes, after writing those tricky Grade 13 exams, I received a message to go to the office to meet Mr. Duke, our vice principal. At first, I cringed a little because I knew him to be a rather stern man of few words and plenty of threatening glares. He'd supervised some of my detentions during my first years of high school.

When I walked into his office, he looked up at me, "Neill, have a chair." I had never been asked to sit with him before. "We'd like to nominate you to attend a United Nations seminar for young people at the University of Waterloo."

"Really?" I asked, not knowing what else to say.

"Yes, your teachers and I have agreed you are the one most likely to benefit from and contribute to this conference, and would be well-suited to represent our school. Do you want to attend?"

"Sure," I answered. I can't remember what else I said—too overwhelmed by the offer.

I'M IN THE MIDDLE WEARING
A SWEATER WITH DIAMOND SHAPES.

A couple of weeks later, I found myself as part of a team of four representing Canada amongst 200 students from Ontario and Quebec. The others were given even more difficult tasks of speaking for foreign countries. I remember many smart counterparts—including some girls so attractive and articulate. I felt inadequate but did my best. We discussed the Cold War and Vietnam, listened to speakers, argued international issues, passed resolutions, and forged new brain cells.

When I returned home, I wrote an article for the town's newspaper, the Elmira Signet. On reviewing what I wrote many years later, I found passages that brought back to me how much I had been affected by this experience:

Canada is a particularly difficult country to represent because we have interests in the Commonwealth, the US and the Soviet Union. The Canadian diplomat's job is to try to keep everyone happy and what can you do if the US disagrees with the UK or the USSR on a certain resolution? The purpose of the seminar is to educate young Canadians to the realities of world government. The UN organization is in crisis, in a point of deadlock where neither the Soviet Union nor the US are willing to say "uncle." However, we must keep in mind that this is only the political side, the part of the organization that is pumped into the newspapers. Behind the headlines, never reported by journalists, lies a vast structure of great importance, servicing mankind in fields of development, human rights and disarmament....For I do believe this organization has a future, perhaps giving us our only hope in a world where great nations continue to squabble, while standing beside their respective control buttons.

In retrospect, I think I had undergone a "sea change" since that autumn evening when I walked into the Young People's meeting. [At the time, I certainly couldn't see into the future—that I would one day work for the United Nations and other international organizations.]

That summer, I labored once again at Dad's factory, assembling Claas Combines imported from Germany—a new line of business the company had taken up. As the days passed, I became increasingly worried about the results of the Grade 13 exams. If I didn't pass all subjects and get a reasonable overall average, I would be stuck in Elmira for another year. Finally, I got a telephone call from the school's secretary who said that the results had arrived. I asked my supervisor for permission to rush to the high school to pick up my envelope. I sat down to study the small slip of paper inside. I had passed all subjects, including algebra, but just barely. Ironically, my highest mark was in chemistry and lowest was in English. That really stank! I had put so much effort into English during the last two years of high school. Later, it was confirmed to me that something was rotten in both the English and algebra exams' preparation and marking systems that year, not worth dwelling on here.

I had already received provisional letters of acceptance from Queens University in Kingston, Carleton

University in Ottawa, and the University of Western Ontario in London, a city located to the west of Elmira. I toyed with the idea of doing science and then medicine at Queens, possibly leading to psychiatry. At the time, my sister Karen and her fiancé were studying nursing and science, respectively, at Queens. With their help, I visited Queens' Faculty of Medicine, including the cadaver dissection lab. To this day, when you mention Queens to me, all I can think of is a cross-section of the head of a woman with a hooked nose. She had been split right through the middle and half of her head floated in a jar of formaldehyde. That sight erased any thoughts I had about going into biology or medicine.

Because of the U.N. conference and the influence of Mr. Huschka, I contemplated studying political science at Carleton, but due to my role model, Al Evans, I was considering psychology as well. The University of Western Ontario had the best psychology program of the three. Besides, I concluded, I could take both psychology and political science in the first year and then decide.

In August, I quit my job at McKee Brothers early to get ready for university and to attend the United Church's Ryerson Camp for young people at Turkey Point on Lake Erie. I'd never returned to such a camp since our hilarious breakout from the United Church summer camp for boys on Lake Huron. Not surprisingly, a lot of the songs, hymns, and prayers remained the same, but I met a number of young people who were searching for answers, like I was, and didn't embrace a simple interpretation of Christianity.

I also met Roy McDonald from London, Ontario, at the camp. He was a small skinny guy with a beard as long as Rabindranath Tagore's and a balding head. He professed to be a Zen Buddhist and a poet. The United Church had become, by then, the most liberal mainstream church in Canada and didn't prohibit this older Zen Buddhist from infiltrating young minds. He seemed so articulate. He showed me another of Alan Watts' books, *Nature, Man and Woman*—advertised on the cover as "a new approach to sexual experience." What could be better because I had none, at least in the full sense of the word. Why start with old approaches?

RECOMMENDED TO ME
AT UNITED CHURCH YOUNG PEOPLE'S CAMP

JANET AND OUR SANDCASTLE.

I got to know Janet at the camp, a beautiful young woman with whom I became close that week. I have a photo of her behind a double-spired sandcastle, which we built together. She's wearing a red and white striped blouse and blue trench coat, almost breaking my camera with her smile.

Unfortunately, or fortunately, I can't really say, she had a steady boyfriend in her hometown and planned to attend another university. Somehow, it didn't matter. I only wanted to live for the moment. I might have written to her a few times after that, but if we had really connected again it could have changed the course of my life. Was it a missed opportunity or just a fleeting relationship that washed away, like our double-spired sandcastle?

On the last day of camp, I walked alone up the high sandhills overlooking Lake Erie to stare at the water and think. I gazed out over the dark blue waves toward the far-off American shore. My readings and discussions with Roy, Janet, and others, which had been so intense, now seemed distant. Other sensations rushed into the vacuum. As I breathed in lake air, I felt my eyes well up in joyful relief. I brushed a mosquito from my neck and felt the cool breeze on my face. I heard waves lapping on the shore, baseball players shouting in the distance, and music from the dining hall record player filtering through the trees. Everything great about life rushed through my soul at once. I realized that the religion I'd been seeking was the unity all around me, and I was a part of it.

Above all, I knew I'd soon be leaving Elmira for good and heading into the next chapter of my life. I finally understood what Bob Dylan meant for me when he sang: *The Times They Are A-Changin'*.

WHAT DID I GET MYSELF INTO?

15

Existential Leaps

The pilot shouted over the din of the airplane engine, "It's time. Get ready!"

I mouthed weakly, "Okay." He seemed to have a smirk on his face, daring me. I don't think he could hear me but he could probably read my dry lips.

Then I tilted my head downwards and to the right. Because the door had been removed, I could see the wheel and the small step, the two places where I had to put my feet, as instructed. In addition, at St. Thomas Parachuting Club near London, Ontario, the trainers taught me how to push off into the air, wait for the shoot to fully open, steer toward the target, and roll when I hit the Earth. That's what I had practiced on the ground during the previous three Saturdays, and it all seemed kind of theoretical, until now.

In 1965, we had to do our first jump solo, although the ripcord for the main chute was attached to the plane so it would open automatically a few seconds after leaping away. As trained, I had fastened a pack containing a smaller safety chute to my chest for self-deployment in case the first one failed. It seemed to me we spent an inordinate amount of time learning how to pack both chutes so we alone would be responsible if they didn't open—a little unnerving. I knew once I stepped out, I couldn't get back in. My trainer told me it would be dangerous to try. I might slip and then be knocked by the passing tail of the plane. I had dreams of something like that happening during a couple of nights before the jump. What a crazy thing to do? Why had I let Bob Kavanagh talk me into it? I had taken up his challenge on a lark.

I blanked out all other thoughts and swung out, grabbing the wing brace and placing my feet firmly. I glanced past my running shoes to the ground, a half mile (805 meters) below. The wind whipped me as I waited for the command to push off. Time seemed to slow down, almost stop.

Then the pilot, holding my small camera, shouted, "Get set... go!"

For a few seconds, black and white checkered patterns passed before my eyes, no time, no space. Images of me as a child, our house, my family, friends, warm blue water, mountains and sun. I floated in infinity— then snap!—as my parachute opened. Perched like a king on a tall tower, I inspected my realm. I remember feeling quite pleased with myself. My whole body vibrated with excitement. Late October's brown fields came into focus below. I breathed in cool pure air.

MAKING MY FIRST "EXISTENTIAL LEAP

I saw the buildings of the airport and remembered how I should pull the strings of the chute to steer toward the red and white target my instructor had placed in a nearby field. It reminded me I had a date with the Earth. But I found it difficult to concentrate on something so specific. I continued to float a little too freely and the wind took me about 100 yards (30.5 meters) off course, right above the tarmac. In the last 15 seconds, I tried to maneuver toward a grassy area, but suddenly my knees buckled and then, "bump!" I forgot to roll onto one leg and side to absorb the shock. A rude welcome back, landing squarely on my ass. Pain shot up my spine.

Bob came running out to greet me, "Great going, Neill." He was that same friend and former student minister. He'd decided not to follow the divinity track and had, instead, enrolled in a master's degree in philosophy at our nearby university. He had convinced me it would be good for me to take such an "existential leap," words I didn't fully understand until I jumped.

I stood up, wincing and holding my back, "Don't feel so great."

"Ya, what happened there?"

"Guess I forgot to do the roll."

"You came down pretty hard."

"The wind blew me off course." I didn't tell him that in my sensation of sailing, I'd lost track of time and space.

Bob said, "Well, it was only your first try. You should do better the next time."

As I hobbled to the club house, I privately wondered if there would be a next time.

Beginners at the club had to start with the old dome-shape chutes—the kind that fill the sky and get caught in trees in World War II movies. These military-style

OLD DOME-SHAPED CHUTES FOR BEGINNERS

chutes fall faster than the newer type that more experienced club members used—the "para-commander," a wider and shallower construction—not completely circular in shape and easier to steer.

For a couple of weeks, it felt uncomfortable to sit. I went home the next weekend, only about 80 miles (131 km) from London, to have our family chiropractor, Dr. Hallman, treat me. He reminded me I had buggered up my back a few years earlier, while lifting a heavy load at Dad's factory. But he said my back should recover. He didn't recommend parachuting as a sport, but seemed to understand the attraction.

A few weeks earlier, I had landed at the nearby University of Western Ontario in London with an equally hard thud, in a psychological sense. My room in the brand-new Sydenham Hall men's residence was small, with no bathroom or sink—only two beds, two desks, and two cupboards in which to store clothes and suitcases. I shared it with Jason, a chap from England, his side to the right as you entered, mine to the left.

From a window in the middle of the outside wall, I could see the new gray stones and small trees lining the courtyard of our residence. Our study chairs were placed back-to-back. If I leaned back far enough, I could see a piece of sky and tree tops. The exterior of the building shouted, "Look at us. We are Ivy League!" But to me, its drab yellow-green curtains and veneer-covered desks answered, "We are mediocrity!"

I had tacked my weekly schedule and important notices to the bulletin board above my desk, carefully

SYDENHAM HALL MEN'S RESIDENCE

arranging my books and notebooks on the shelf for easy access. I always made my bed and put away my clothes. I'll admit I was fastidious in those days. My roommate was not.

Jason's side looked like the aftermath of a battle: dirty clothes strewn all over the bed and floor—a lonely shoe here, a lost sock there. His desktop remained scattered with unused books and scraps of paper. From the photos of his parents and sister, tacked haphazardly to his bulletin board, I had the impression he came from an upper middle-class family who had banished him to "the colonies" in mild hope of a miraculous reformation.

TWO SOLITUDES

Jason's chief concern appeared to be "getting sloshed" and "banging girls." He spoke with a clipped accent, kind of like the Beatles, but more refined, stringing one cliché after another: "You wouldn't believe this chick I met, a beautiful piece, Neill. I didn't know Canada had so much to offer. Wow, is she hot in bed!"

Sometimes Jason spoke too fast and I couldn't understand him. I'd only ask him to repeat himself if I felt he said something mildly important. Otherwise, I would only smile. I didn't want to encourage a conversation on some subject in which I had no interest. I remembered such talk with my old gang in Elmira—most of it just bragging.

Jason would return in the middle of the night and sleep deeply into the day. Then he'd get up for afternoon classes in order to meet up with "chicks" and start the cycle over again. Our room functioned like a train platform where two strangers meet each other daily, engage in a few pleasantries, and then continue on their separate journeys.

Western's campus is perched on a hill—gray stone buildings bordered by the Thames River and the city. At the time, it was dominated by the spires of University and Middlesex Colleges—an imitation of Oxford or Cambridge. During fall orientation for freshmen, called "frosh week," I witnessed a lot of ritual hazing. Western's social life mimicked America's—fraternities, sororities, and their drinking parties. The tension in the air involved fitting in and getting laid. I had no interest

MIDDLESEX COLLEGE WITH
ITS MEDIUM SIZE PHALLIC SYMBOL

in joining such "Greek gangs." I considered them to be immature nonsense. I had already experienced enough of adolescent life.

When I arrived at Sydenham Hall, I spotted an unusual looking guy sitting alone in our residence's cafeteria. He had very dark skin and wore a white shirt with tie and jacket. I sat down at his table and said, "Hello, I'm Neill McKee, first year. What's your name?"

He looked a little surprised to be addressed so directly but replied in very proper English, "My name is Naison Mawande and I am from Southern Rhodesia."

I recalled discussions about South Africa and apartheid at the U.N. seminar I had attended during the summer, but didn't know much about Southern Rhodesia. He engaged me in an interesting conversation. We talked about why he came to study and his dreams of helping to solve the problems in his country. He was doing a Ph.D. in political science and he planned to return home to make a difference for his people.

Naison and I met at many mealtimes and, among other things, traded stories of our childhoods—my adventures in Elmira and my escapes while fishing and exploring the woods and river valleys of Ontario; his hikes through African plains and forests while caring for his family's herds of goats and cattle. As we talked, my thoughts drifted from 1965 back to those strange shapes on the hill and our playing "Africa" with the Steed girls.

In November of my first term at Western, the white rulers of Naison's country declared unilateral independence from Britain in order to maintain domination of the black population. The whites wanted to stop their political advancement, including their right to vote.

Naison and I discussed similar conflict between blacks and whites in the U.S.'s southern states. I lived through weekly developments with him. He worried about his country's future, and his own.

Returning to my room after talks with Naison, I would sometimes encounter shaving cream riots. I had to dodge streams of white foam. The participants darted in and out of doors and up and down the halls, like commandos in training. On some nights, they held rowdy pizza and beer parties. I would either go to the library to study or put on a record and turn the volume up, blotting out their antics. These guys, I guessed, had only recently broken out of surveillance by overprotective parents. They hadn't known the freedom I had experienced at home.

I think Naison stayed at Sydenham Hall because it offered all of the services that he might find more difficult and time-consuming to navigate if he had taken a private apartment. He never commented on the juvenile behavior of our fellow residents, but he told me it helped him gain insight into Canadian culture. I tried to convince him this was not really our culture, only a passing youthful stage. But I'm not sure he believed me or that I believed what I was telling him.

I brought Naison home to Elmira to experience a Canadian Christmas and our friendship deepened. My parents found him delightful, so polite and refined. They made him feel at home as much as possible, and perhaps it helped him appreciate our culture a little more.

My talks with Naison led me to more seriously consider politics as a possibility for specialization; however, from the very first day of my Political Science 101 course,

NAISON WITH THE MCKEE'S AT CHRISTMAS

the professor turned me off. He would walk into class, open his text book and proceed to read page-after-page of dry Canadian constitutional history in a monotone voice. His greatest expression consisted of short grunts to clear his throat and slight shifts of his right shoulder, when he turned a page—like an involuntary muscle tic. The class could have been good for discussion, especially about Quebec, where the FLQ continued to set off bombs, but the professor seldom looked up at his snoozing students. English Canada slept as Quebec rose up in protest.

My university courses were a breeze compared to Grade 13. As in senior high school, I found English class to be the most engaging, especially all the satire in Chaucer's *Canterbury Tales* and the wit and dark images in T.S. Eliot's long poem, *The Waste Land*. I also had to take one year of a foreign language and my French professor taught Voltaire's *Candide* like Bill Exley taught

English. I loved the irony in Candide's pronouncements that, "All is for the best in the best of all possible worlds." This sure beat the French literature I had to endure in high school, but these classes never contributed to my learning to speak French either.

Psychology stirred some interest in me, especially the parts on abnormal behavior. I had known people with similar symptoms, especially neurotics. But the stimulus-response paradigm seemed too dry and mechanical—findings mainly based on experiments with rats running through mazes.

Periodically, I had a coffee or a meal with Bob, who had entered a period of intellectual struggle with existentialism, especially while studying Kierkegaard. Put simply, existentialism is a philosophical movement grounded in our subjective experiences in space and time, rather than metaphysical speculation or verifiable empirical observations about reality, the meaning of life, or the existence of God. Some say it is more a cultural and literary movement rather than a branch of philosophy. I had read a little of Kierkegaard's *Fear and Trembling*, especially on being in a relationship with God. Bob had been working through this in a personal way; whereas, I already had become some kind of universalist and claimed no personal relationship with an all-powerful God. Claims of personal and national relationships with God had already caused so many conflicts and wars throughout history: Christians versus Jews, Jews versus Muslims, Muslims versus Christians, and on and on.

I preferred to study existentialism in the literature we read in French class: Albert Camus' *L'Etranger* and Jean

Paul Sartre's *Nausea*. I started writing an essay, which I called "Beyond Nausea," but ironically never got beyond the introduction.

Sometimes I would bump into Roy McDonald in one of the campus cafeterias. We had discussed Zen Buddhism at the United Church Young People's camp in the summer. I came to comprehend that Judeo-Christian thought strives to understand the nature of God, though it neglects the nature of humanity and our connection with nature itself. On the other hand, Zen Buddhists regard nature as an organic whole within which man is fully integrated. That's what I came to believe.

As I got to know Roy a little better, I learned he had become a regular fixture on campus, but wasn't a registered student. He loved to talk about Zen and spiritualism in general, especially its relationship to sex. By then I'd completed Alan Watts' books, *Nature, Man and Woman*, recommended by Roy. Although around 40 years old, he continued to live with his mother. He didn't have a job but wrote a bit of poetry. He gave me one of his self-published books. Most of the time he hung out in cafeterias to have "deep conversations" with students, especially beautiful young women. The campus overflowed with them, so our conversations were frequently interrupted by his "Zen moments," as I secretly called them, when he got so worked up that he seemed to go off in his pants.

A lot of people called Roy a "phony" and avoided him. I had been through all that "Holden Caufield stuff" and thought Roy was just being Roy. But as the year progressed, I also tried to avoid him and his "Zen moments." [To my surprise, when I was writing this book, my high school English teacher, Bill Exley (who is also one of the founders and musicians of the now world-famous Nihilist Spasm Band), told me what happened to Roy: "He became quite well-known in London as he got older, busking on Richmond Row, attending many of our Nihilist annual picnics, and other London festivals….When Roy died in early 2018, very many people came to his funeral, including local dignitaries, and also to a tribute event for him at Covent Garden Market, where local officials gave speeches and some young people spoke about how he had changed their lives for the better. I also gave a speech at both events."

When I read Bill's words, I searched further and found that two of Roy McDonald's books were published by Ergo Publications: a long pun-poem, *The Answer Questioned* (1970) and *Living: A London Journal* (1978)—a detailed account of a week of Roy's life. I came to realize how many people he influenced, besides me, and that he had been one of the original counter-culture rebels fighting against the conformist culture I hated at Western.]

I dated a few different girls at Western but never became attached to any of them. I can vaguely recall one who loved pomegranate seeds. I have a photo of another with me in my album from that year, but her name is missing. Her hair is piled high in a bee-hive, and we're all dressed up for the Sydenham Hall dinner and dance.

I asked Ruth to send me a photo of herself in a pink and white dress with her hair also in a bee-hive, taken on the evening she came with me to my Grade 13 graduation dinner and dance. I kept in touch with

SYDENHAM HALL FORMAL 1966.

ME WITH MYSTERY WOMAN   RUTH IN 1965

her in Elmira by mail, and met her when I went home at Christmas. She planned to start at Western the next year, but we agreed we wouldn't be a couple, however awkward it might become. We talked about our backgrounds being too similar and thought we might become a crutch for one another, which would limit our new experiences. I guess I really wanted to remain a "kid on the go," not tied down to anyone, and maybe she felt the same.

I pinned both photos to the bulletin board in my room. Although I was happy to have such memorabilia, in truth, I was lonely and discontented at Western. I listened a lot to Dave Brubeck's LP, *Time Out*. I didn't really get into the full musical movement of the time but had an LP of The Beatles, and another by Marianne Faithful singing *As Tears Go By*. I would often go to the usually empty residence lounge to play my copy of

Rachmaninoff's *Piano Concerto No. 2,* which would take me on an emotional, imagined trip to undefined, far-away places—anywhere but Western.

In March during "Slack Week" (our name for "Spring Break"), Bob and I headed to Wawa, Ontario, an iron ore mining community about 560 miles (901 km) due north of Toronto. Our mutual Elmira friends Wally and Jeanette Panagapka had moved there to teach school and we wanted to do some snowmobiling and have a good time with them and their kids for a few days.

We took a bus from London through Toronto. Leaving Toronto, Bob took a seat in the back to read or stretch out and sleep. I sat alone. Moments before pulling out of the

SKIDOOING ON LAKE WAWA

station, a woman boarded and sat beside me. Jennifer was shapely and quite attractive. She wore strong perfume, heavy make-up, and she smoked.

As we rolled through the day and into the evening, her story unfolded. She had recently been released from a famous old prison called "Don Jail" in Toronto. She said, "I'm heading to Calgary, or maybe I'll go to Vancouver."

I asked, "What's the attraction?"

"Don't know," she said. "Need a change of scenery after staring at a wall for months. I hear the Rockies are beautiful. Never been there. Have you?"

"One time when I was a kid," I replied. "It's the best part of Canada."

I listened attentively, like a psychology student should do, injecting a few questions once in a while, gently counseling her on her future. I think she said she had been sentenced for something drug-related, possibly prostitution as well. Whatever the crime, she had been in too long. As the sun went down, she leaned more and more on me—obviously horny. This made psychological counseling somewhat difficult in the dark. She put her fake fur coat over our laps and began to rub my crotch. As we rubbed and rumbled northwards into the night, I experienced the most pleasurable bus ride I had ever taken.

We finally reached the bus stop at Wawa, the point at which the Trans-Canada Highway begins to gradually bend westward over the top of Lake Superior. Bob and I invited Jennifer to a brief and awkward coffee in the restaurant with Wally, who had come to meet us. Wally might have wondered what had happened between me and this woman but said nothing, being a non-judgmental person. There was a short debate about whether she should stay with us for a while to receive more "counseling." Then I walked Jennifer to the bus and said goodbye, never to see her again.

I watched Jennifer's bus depart and turn right, heading northwest on the Trans-Canada Highway. From my childhood, I had heard stories of my uncles going "out West" as young men to find their futures. By then my brother Glen had also done just that. After quitting school in Grade 10, he had worked for McKee Brothers for a while. Then he ventured out West to Red Deer, Alberta, to work for Uncle Jim. There, he realized he was at a dead end, so he returned home to complete Grade 12 in a crash course, followed by business school, where he became the student president. Later, he married an Elmira girl and studied to become a successful quality control engineer.

I knew that going out West could be transformational. Even my mentor Al Evans had decided to change his course in life when he was chasing a criminal across the prairies in Saskatchewan. So, when I saw Jennifer's bus disappear from sight, I felt a deep yearning to go in the same direction.

16

Call of the Wild Goose

At the end of my year at Western, I executed another jump—bright sun reflected off green fields mixed with deep brown patches. The earth below seemed like a welcoming soft quilt. Having some fun, the guys in the parachute club put the target in a muddy field and I aimed in its general direction. But I glided over it, maneuvering my chute to a strip of dry grass where I performed a proper roll—a perfect ending to an imperfect first year at university.

A week later, I found myself plunging downward again. For the first few seconds I floated, and then reality hit as I began counting different forms of the root word "fuck," such as, "fucking," "fucked," "fucked-up," and "fuck-face" coming from the man beside me. He reached 17 such utterances by the time we stopped halfway down, where he got off.

ALGOMA IRON ORE MINE, WAWA, ONTARIO

As we continued the descent, conversational cursing by others resumed. Finally, we arrived at my level, the bottom, 2,066 feet (630 meters) underground. It was May, and I had returned to Wawa for the summer to work at Algoma, an iron ore mine.

I walked out into the shadowy gloom with a small group of miners. One guy took me to my workstation, saying, "Stand here until Jack comes and shows you what to do."

I followed his order and watched cast iron buckets swinging in on a thick cable, pausing while ore poured into them, then swinging out.

Eventually, Jack came along and pointed to a shovel and a broom, saying, "Your job is to clean up that overspill."

"What do you mean?" I asked.

Jack smirked and shouted above the racket all around us, "You go in there and throw the spill back into the buckets when they come in and stop."

"Holy shit! Are you kidding?"

"No joke. You only have a short time for each cleanup. See the controller up there. He's Ben."

I looked up through the dusty air at a dirty window and saw Ben smiling and waving at me. I imagined him to be saying something like, *Yes, you sucker. Stay down there and get the fuck to work.*

They never bothered to explain how the system operated. I figured it out by myself. The miners blasted out and gathered the iron ore from mine shafts above us. They then sent it down various chutes to this loading point. The buckets, weighing about one ton each, somehow swung into the dock on a cable system every 30

AT THE BOTTOM OF THE PIT

225

seconds to be filled with two tons of ore in one sudden thundering download. Then they swung out to start the long journey up to the surface.

My job sounded simple, as described by Jack, but I only had about 20 seconds to complete my duty after each download. I had to calculate precisely, otherwise my head would meet up with one of the buckets. I surmised the puny fiberglass safety helmet I had been issued wouldn't offer much protection. I didn't trust Ben's degree of control. I concluded footwork was crucial for survival. But after a few hours, my legs started to drag.

This daily dance with death continued for about two weeks—the most dangerous work I had ever done. In comparison, working in my dad's factory had been a piece of cake. But my fellow miners only made jokes about it. At times, I wondered if Ben deliberately allowed more ore to spill on purpose. Maybe they had all begun their mining careers at this workstation—literally and figuratively the bottom of the pit.

One morning, while I was sweating away at my mindless task, Jack came up to me with another summer student employee. "This fellow's going to take your place," he shouted into my ear. "They want you up in the personnel office."

"Really? What for?" I asked. Jack shrugged.

As I made my way to the elevator, I wondered if they intended to fire me. Not up to the mark? When I entered the personnel office, they ushered me into the medical section. Maybe they thought I wasn't fit. In spite of the horrendous task I had to perform, I felt fine. In fact, all the shoveling and footwork had strengthened my muscles considerably.

A guy in a white coat greeted me and asked me to sit down. I thought to myself, *White coat! This is getting serious.* He pulled out some papers and began to talk, "We're going to reassign you to a different position. I've reviewed your records and I see a letter from a chiropractor. You had a back injury last year. How did it happen?"

"A parachuting club. I forgot to roll properly when I hit the ground."

"Wow!" The guy said. "You take chances."

"But I learned and made a perfect roll the second time."

"That's great," he said. "But we can't take a chance on further injury. You're going to work in the maintenance office."

"What's the job involve?" I asked.

"Paperwork and maybe some inspections."

Salvation, I thought.

Another guy marched me over to the maintenance office, where I learned about my new job. They showed me how to handle cards that were placed in different slots. These cards ordered equipment maintenance checks and repairs, or inspection of repairs, to be carried out by millwrights. Perhaps this new task allowed for my physical survival, but I soon found out it posed a real threat to my mental health.

After a few weeks, I came to realize the interchanges between the inspectors and office workers were excellent material for an absurdist play, which I began to write. The cards shifted ever so slightly—the orders here, the completions there—blending with my co-workers' utterances and banter: "L-16 is okay now." "That asshole is back again." "The Red Sox are leading ten to five. "Time to make my rounds." "Could sure use a cold beer right now." "God, is it only 3:30?" "It's elevator seven again." "You screwed up!" "Go fuck yourself." "No, you can take a flying fuck!" "Time to check L-20." "Fred ought to be fired; doesn't know his ass from a hole in the ground."

Their form of communication, short utterances and grunts in place of considered thought, made my questions and suggestions on possible improvements to my card shuffling function, fruitless. After all, I was only a summer worker and wouldn't understand why a particular task had to be done in a particular way. After a number of unsuccessful proposals for reform, I decided I'd better stick to completing my assigned work and just punch the clock. For my sanity, I began to think of it as a board game, which I would eventually figure out, at least by the end of the summer. It would all be in my playscript.

In contrast, I loved the longer summer evenings in Wawa, the Ojibwe word for "call of the wild goose," so I was told. This interpretation probably came from Henry Wadsworth Longfellow's poem, *The Song of Hiawatha*, which contains this verse:

> All the wild-fowl sang them to him,
> In the moorlands and the fen-lands,
> In the melancholy marshes;
> Chetowaik, the plover, sang them,
> Mahng, the loon, the wild-goose, Wawa,
> The blue heron, the Shuh-shuh-gah,
> And the grouse, the Mushkodasa!

WAWA GOOSE STATUE ON THE TRANS-CANADA HIGHWAY

Wewe is the actual Ojibwe word and it means "snow goose" rather than "Canada goose," which is *nika* in this native language. The town council, not worrying too much about inaccurate cultural appropriation, placed a large statue of a Canada goose facing the western horizon, wings spread wide, beckoning travelers on the TransCanada highway to stop.

In Wawa, I had adequate time to think, read, and write letters to friends, or work on more of my terrible poetry, as well as my attempted absurdist play, which I never finished. Claude Gastonguay and Robert Corcoran from Sherbrooke, Quebec, boarded with me at the Panagapkas' place, while they went to southern Ontario for summer courses. On weekends, Claude, Robert, and I fished together while discussing French-English relations in our country. I tried my poor French on them and we laughed at what I'd been taught, as compared to their French.

CLAUDE GASTONGUAY AND ROBERT CORCORAN

Claude descended from some of the first French set-tlers of the St. Lawrence Valley, who arrived in the early 1600s, 200 years before the British conquest. Robert, who pronounced his name "Ro-bare Cor-ca-rán," descended from Irish Catholics who had assimilated and spoke French as their first language. We talked about the on-go-ing violence in Quebec by the FLQ, and the reasons for it. These talks and our growing friendship gave me new hope for our country, and helped erase from memory my boring poli-sci 101 experience at Western.

During my sojourn in Wawa, I dated a girl by the name of Cheryl a few times—a cousin of a girl I had met at Western. I took her canoeing on Lake Wawa. While the forest to the east of the town had been killed off by sul-fur and other by-products of iron ore mining and refin-ing, the land to the west remained picturesque: stately evergreens and crystal blue lakes—great for canoeing, as long as you covered your skin with plenty of mosquito repellent. But no sparks flew between Cheryl and me.

LAKE WAWA

She stared blankly when I talked about philosophy and writing my absurdist play on life in the maintenance office. Her father was one of the supervisors at the mine and provided for her university education—no joking matter, I guess.

In July, an important letter arrived from the University of Calgary. After March break in Wawa, I had decided Western was definitely not for me. I didn't see much of Bob, and I hadn't grown attached to any other friends, male or female, except Naison. But he would be finishing his studies that year and he planned to return home to join the fight for his people's freedom. [That didn't happen right away, for I met him again in Toronto in 1972, when he was raising funds for the struggle against the white racist Rhodesian government. It lasted until the majority blacks won a protracted bush war for self-rule in 1980, when the nation of Zimbabwe was born.]

The prospect of three more years at Western seemed increasingly claustrophobic to me. I had looked up all the courses at universities in the western part of Canada and found the University of Calgary best matched to carry forward all my course credits.

In mid-August, I picked up my last paycheck from Algoma. In the morning, I boarded a small plane for Toronto. As we took off, I saw the café and bus stop where I had said goodbye to that mysterious woman Jennifer five months earlier. In a strange way, she'd been a catalyst for my move. I could see Wawa's goose getting smaller as I began my flight home, where I packed and, a few days later, boarded a westward-bound train in Toronto for Calgary.

Finally, I was on my way out West toward open spaces below vast blue skies, towering mountains, fresh winds, and the possibility of a completely new beginning.

17
A Chinook Wind Arrives

For most of an hour, I had been sitting safely in the seats high above the apron stage, watching the proceedings. Suddenly the director barked instructions my way.

"You in the gray sweater, come and read this!"

Reluctantly, I walked down the stairs and onto the stage, took the script, and began to read.

"Now with more emotion!" he ordered.

I tried again. The director scratched his head, gave me some more lines, and asked me to move around as I read. After a few more minutes of this, he told his assistant to take my name and number. I went back to the safety of my observation post to watch the remaining auditions—especially the talented and beautiful young women.

It was early September 1966 and I had arrived at the University of Calgary the day before. I had been exploring my new campus when I saw the sign for auditions.

I never had any great interest in theater and no acting experience at all. I had only intended to watch.

The next day, I received a call at my residence from Professor Mitchell's assistant, Hedy, who gave me the time and place to show up for rehearsals. He had cast me as Bonario in *Volpone*, a play set in Venice and written by Ben Jonson, a contemporary of Shakespeare. Bonario, as his name suggests, is a good guy amongst parasites, fools, and the lecherous old man Volpone. I had to save the fair damsel Celia from his designs on her virtue.

In the play, Volpone finds a way to be alone with Celia and demands, "Yield, or I'll force thee."

One hand to her adequate bosom, Celia cries, "Oh! Just God!"

Leering with delight at her breasts, Volpone replies, "In vain!"

BONARIO AND CELIA IN *VOLPONE*

From a balcony, I had to leap down to the rescue in the nick of time, like a 17th century Batman, shouting my all-important lines:

"Forbear, foul ravisher! Libidinous swine! Free the forced lady or thou diest, imposter."

After this gallant speech, I spirited Celia away to safety, which I didn't mind doing night-after-night, because the voluptuous drama major Patricia played Celia.

I must confess, even after many nights of rehearsal and sarcastic prodding by Professor Mitchell, my acting remained pretty wooden. At first I had stage fright, especially the fear of forgetting my lines, so I pounded them into my brain. This worked well. On opening night, the Calgary Herald reviewer didn't pan me, as I had expected.

Next, the department cast me as the sadistic drum major in Georg Büchner's *Woyzeck*, an expressionistic German tragedy set in the 1800s, in which I had to beat up the main character, the lowly soldier Woyzeck, played by my friend Wes Tritter. In the script, Woyzeck is emotionally wounded by an unfaithful mistress, whom the drum major seduces. I had to fight with Woyzeck, and Wes complained I really hurt him sometimes with my fake blows. This time the newspaper critic called me "ferociously effective"—quite a surprise. I thought maybe the reviewer had been dozing and had woken up with our shouts when I pretended to punch Wes. But a good review it was and it really helped cement my position as part of the drama gang.

During the January to April semester of 1967, the drama department cast me in my final role, "Indian Joe," a minor character in *The Ottawa Man*. The playwright

DRUM MAJOR AND WOYZECK IN *WOYZECK*

was Mavor Moore—a popular western Canadian writer, producer, actor, critic, and educator at the time. Moore had adapted his work from Nikolai Gogol's, *The Inspector General*, a Russian play.

In the story, Indian Joe is a servant of the local mayor. Joe silently observes all the corruption going on in the community. I had no lines at all, probably a comment by the playwright on the place Canada's indigenous people had in society. In a twist at the end, Indian Joe is revealed as a federal policeman who has gathered all the evidence needed for prosecution of corrupt officials, including the mayor. My part in this play was the least consequential of the three I acted in, but it probably better matched my acting talent—a good prop.

At the time, the drama department classrooms and

theater stood in the center of the campus, a gleaming set of new buildings on the western side of the city, without the creeping ivy or pseudo-Oxford stone walls of the University of Western Ontario. On a very clear day, the Rocky Mountains could be seen on the horizon from our all-male residence, Rundle Hall, and from the dining hall. The buildings screamed "here and now," a mid-century architect's dream.

Wasfi Youssef agreed. The day I arrived, the residence administrative clerk asked me if I had any preference for a roommate. I didn't want another juvenile sex fiend and budding alcoholic like Jason at Western, and I knew no other students in Calgary. I looked down the list and saw his name and country of origin,

WASFI YOUSSEF, 1967

"Egypt." When we met later that day, Wasfi told me he was a Ph.D. student in civil engineering. Immediately, saving the pyramids came to my mind—a stereotypical thought on my part. In fact, he was trying to solve a specific problem of slab-column connections in reinforced concrete. He never lectured me on it, knowing I probably wouldn't be interested. He had already completed his master's degree in Egypt and had three years of experience building housing for Russian engineers and the Egyptians who worked on the Upper Nile River's Aswan Dam. He had helped complete a complex of 65 buildings, but remained modest, never boasting about his accomplishments.

Later, Wasfi told me he found out he had been entitled to a private room in our university residence. When he arrived in Calgary, the residence clerk asked him what year he was in and he replied "first," but modestly didn't explain "first year doctorate." After we met, he decided to stay put, an honor for me.

Wasfi came from Egypt's Copt community, one of the oldest Christian cultures in the world. His first language was Arabic but he insisted he was not an Arab. We talked a lot, went for meals together, and became good friends. We listened to his LPs by a modern and popular female Arabic signer, Fairuz, who came from the Lebanese Christian Maronite community. For the first time, I felt the emotional allure of the East when I heard her album, *An Evening in Beirut*. At the time, travel writers called Beirut "the jewel of the Orient"—a romantic destination for many.

Through Wasfi, I got to know Gamil Sabry, also a Copt, and Sherif Aggor, a Muslim Egyptian, as well as other foreign students. Wasfi had an infectious laugh and we roared together once we started telling stories. He also became a hit with my new drama student friends, who would come to visit our room more frequently as the year progressed. They were some of the only guys we could relate to. As at Western, I witnessed shaving cream fights and other juvenile antics. Some evenings the male students launched "panty raids" on the girls' residence, a twin tower about 100 yards (30.5 meters) away. They'd dash into women's rooms to steal underwear. I never witnessed such exploits but heard about them when the guys boasted in the washroom the next morning.

Some of the drama students wanted my advice on personal matters, specifically their sexual identity and feelings of alienation. I spent many hours listening to their problems, trying to make them feel more comfortable with themselves. They came to talk to me, knowing I was a psychology student—my only credentials apart from being a good listener. I sometimes caught myself playing Al Evans, my psychologist-minister friend from Elmira.

In my second year (first year at Calgary), I continued to think clinical psychology would be my career choice. However, like at Western, behaviorists dominated the psychology department. Many had come from the U.S. They believed the human brain to be an unknowable black box—only the nexus of responses to stimuli. I took a couple of courses in abnormal psychology, which didn't offer any new skills in counseling my friends. During the 1960s, most people summed up my drama friends' problems in the simplistic dichotomy, "queer" versus "normal." We never used the term "gay" at the time. Looking back, I never thought of my friends as abnormal. I'd read many people, including women, had homosexual tendencies to different degrees—a much larger percentage of the population than popularly believed in 1967.

In my studies at Calgary, I became familiar with psychological tests, survey methods, and scales. I did particularly well in a paper I researched and wrote for my survey class, titled, "Authoritarianism, Anomie and Other Factors in Prejudice Towards French Canadians." I had interest in the subject after spending time with Claude and Robert in Wawa, and remembering some of the negative talk about French Canadians back in Elmira, especially by the guys in Dad's factory. But the methodology I had to follow in this investigation, with a sample of 100 university students as subjects, only involved statistical analysis of multiple-choice responses. What was really going on inside an individual's head was of no consequence because it couldn't be scientifically observed or measured. I was more interested in uncovering the feelings and anxieties people experience through in-depth interviews, and there were no such courses offered at the undergraduate level.

In the summer of 1967 I returned to Ontario, where I worked as an orderly on the 3:00 p.m. to 11:00 p.m. shift at Homewood Sanitarium, a private mental hospital in Guelph, a city not far from Elmira. The inmates I helped to look after consisted of both voluntary admissions and involuntary committals for a wide variety of problems. In the male ward where I worked, catatonic schizophrenic patients stood like statues against the walls, while others sometimes became so agitated, they

ZAPPING A PATIENT'S FRONTAL CORTEX

had to be restrained in straitjackets and heavily sedated. For three months, I fed them, cleaned up their urine and fecal accidents, and helped to strap some down for electric shock treatments, watching them convulse as the current passed through their brains in a desperate but obviously unscientific attempt to rearrange some cells for the better.

I also met patients with whom I could have ordinary conversations. For example, I had talks with an author from Toronto who had written books depicting life in a poor Toronto neighborhood during the Great Depression. He came from an impoverished background himself and had lived the life he wrote about—rare for writers at the time. During the summer, he twice committed himself to Homewood to dry out from alcohol addiction. He told me he knew he'd be back again and again, and that seemed kind of hopeless.

I worked under the command of an orderly who had been on the job for over 30 years. Every evening, he would ask us to prepare a variety of sandwiches, such as seven and a half peanut butter and jelly, six and a half salmon, plus five and a quarter baloney. He ordered us to start this task at precisely 7:10 p.m. for service at 7:45 p.m. because, he insisted, "That is what we always do and what the patients expect." He claimed that variation from his prescriptions would cause chaos.

I'm exaggerating somewhat, but after a few weeks on the job, I privately concluded the hospital's rules and regulations contributed to the patients' problems, helping to ensure a high return rate. Our institutionalized patients were not learning how to deal with the unpredictability of the outside world.

In off hours, with my newly acquired acting skills, I found myself playing both patients and orderlies for the entertainment of family and friends. I impersonated one guy who suffered from schizophrenia, the son of a rich factory-owning family from Kitchener. I had the job of taking him outside for short walks and to sit under a tree. He would point to my lawn chair and repeat over and over, "McKee, McKee, McKee. You see that chair, McKee? That's my grandfather's chair, McKee. Can you fill that chair, McKee?"

With each utterance of my name, he would swat the right side of his head, which had become bald— evidence of an uncontrolled behavioral affliction. My facial expressions, voice, and imitation of his flailing arm drew much laughter, though I privately began to wonder about my lack of empathy for a career in clinical psychology.

When I returned to Calgary in September of 1967, my reservations about psychology began to build even more. Because of my good marks the year before, the department offered me a job in the lab as a research assistant. But I became less and less interested in helping with the game of running rats through mazes and capturing their responses on statistical charts. To become a clinical psychologist, I figured I would have had to be enthusiastic about such work for the next six years, completing a master's degree, and then a Ph.D.

During this year, I took an apartment near the university with Jon, a drama major. He demonstrated a unique capacity to analyze plays, movies, and people's behavior. He knew lines from plays and musicals and would act these out and sing with spontaneity. I missed acting but had no time for it.

I made up for that vacuum by taking a third-year playwriting course. I believe Professor Mitchell, head of the department, allowed me into the class without the usual prerequisites because I had stepped up to the plate to act in three plays for him the previous year. I wrote papers on the playwrights Ibsen, Goethe, Brecht, Beckett, O'Neill, and Miller and tried my own hand at writing one act plays: "The Chess Game," "The True North Strong and Free," and "The Seminary Priest"— all preachy pieces. Professor Mitchell called my writing "Presbyterian." I knew this rang true.

I continued my interest in philosophy, taking a course in epistemology (theory of knowledge), which covered some of the thoughts of Descartes, Locke, Kant, and Berkeley before moving on to Wittgenstein and G.

E. Moore. I found Moore's *A Defense of Common Sense,* attractive because it seemed to refute a lot of those earlier philosophers' theories on perception and reality, pinning what we really know to the common sense spoken in everyday language. I became good at imitating our brainy professor from the U.K. giving a lecture on Moore:

> When Person A says he sees a pine tree, he is not just speculating about certain visual stimuli reaching his corneas, he is stating that indeed a pine tree stands before him. That is to say, when Person A stands before a pine tree and utters the words, 'I see a pine tree' there can be no doubt that he means a certain composite of organic matter, which he gives the label 'pine tree,' is indeed displayed before him, and if Person B stands beside Person A with open eyes and also exclaims the same, we can assume that it is correct to say that a pine tree stands before both Person A and Person B at that moment.

I wrote a paper titled, "Wittgenstein and Language Games," which purported to be an in-depth investigation of the conflicts between that philosopher's views and G. E. Moore's positions. But increasingly, my efforts seemed to me like conversations from the Theatre of the Absurd. I wondered whether the study of such philosophy had inspired Samuel Beckett to write the play *Waiting for Godot,* which I studied in my playwriting course. I became pretty good at reciting lines from that play as well, to entertain my friends. Those absurd conversations reminded me of my job in the maintenance office of the iron ore mine in Wawa during the summer of 1966.

Hanging out with some of the drama guys had its downside. The beautiful female drama students may have thought I had homosexual tendencies. Once, I dated the lovely Patricia, who had played Celia in *Volpone*, but made little progress.

I spent a lot of time in the cafeteria talking to Sherry, a stunning dark-haired and physically well-endowed young woman, full of expression. She had become a Mormon and planned to marry a guy who lived in Utah. She told me she would be moving there as soon as she finished her degree in education. We even talked about the possibility she could become one wife among others. I found her confidence (or naiveté) about entering this strange world quite amazing.

I also dated a Chinese girl from Singapore, a newly independent country, which I had to look up on a map. It had been part of another new country, Malaysia, for only two years and then decided to "go it alone" in 1965. We talked a lot about culture and family. She said her family practiced Buddhism but she didn't seem to know anything about Buddhist thought or Eastern philosophy. She couldn't wait to complete her degree and return to her island home and family. Our friendship never approached being romantic, though it did re-ignite my interest in Zen Buddhism. For a while, I investigated taking a master's degree in East Asian studies.

My dabbling in psychology, philosophy, and drama had not propelled me in any certain direction. At the time, we had the option of taking a three-year general B.A. instead of a four-year honors B.A. I thought about it and rationalized that Ontario's Grade 13 was tougher than my first year at university, and besides, Alberta's secondary education system only went up to Grade 12. Why torture myself and continue for another year when I didn't know what I wanted to do with my life? So, I went with the three-year option.

My continued interest in the Far East led me to apply to the United Church of Canada's Board of World Missions to teach English in Japan. Al Evans arranged an interview in Toronto during Christmas break. But in this crucial session, I probably sabotaged my own application by saying something like, "Christ, Buddha, and Mohammed are all equal manifestations of 'the godhead.'"

After I returned to Calgary, the United Church flew me to Vancouver for a psychological assessment using, for example, the Rorschach inkblot test. I had studied the tests they administered on me in psychology classes and had read the beginnings of debates on their validity, especially for use in predicting behavior outside of white North American culture. But I didn't mind flying over the Rocky Mountains for this. Their continued interest in me was a positive sign.

A few weeks after returning to Calgary, I received a rejection letter, claiming I had a high risk of suffering from cultural shock. I quickly concluded what they really feared was the "theological shock" I might inflict on a church school or congregation in Japan. Despite this rejection, my interest in teaching abroad was whetted.

In the dead of the Albertan winter, I began to get depressed about my future. It felt like I kept hitting a brick wall. One morning after a heavy snowfall, while walking to class I saw a McKee Brothers' snowblower mounted on

MCKEE SNOWBLOWER AT WORK

a tractor, clearing the campus. I had a moment of regret. Had I made the right choice in forsaking my father's business back in Ontario? But the feeling didn't last. I remembered his words, "Business and family don't mix." Nor did it make any sense to look backwards. No matter what the future might bring, I'd go with the flow.

Then a few days later, just by chance, I saw a poster on campus. I walked deliberately into the office indicated and wrote out an application for a two-year teaching assignment with CUSO, Canadian University Service Overseas. I ticked off "Asia" as my preferred destination.

One morning the following week, when I was walking to campus for the interview with CUSO, the world had changed. A yellow arch of cloud had formed between the distant Rocky Mountains and the city below, dissolving at its far edges into salmon pink and orange.

A chinook wind had arrived. Students hurried to their classes, carrying their coats and books while negotiating large puddles created by the melting snow. You could see it in the way they moved, the sudden energy in their steps and interactions, some pointing, some with their heads turned upwards and westwards toward the arch, which separated winter, above, from the warm Pacific wind flowing eastwardly, below. My frozen path to a clear future also began to melt.

About three weeks after the chinook, a letter from CUSO arrived. I had been accepted and would be going to Asia. A month or so later, I received another letter which stated they were sending me to teach high school in Sabah, Malaysia, on the Southeast Asian island of Borneo.

Winter had returned to Calgary, but the warmth of the chinook remained deep within me.

Postscript: Closing the Circle

On Saturday of Labor Day weekend in 2017, I accompanied my cousin David Neill, and his wife Scarlett, to watch the longest gay pride parade I'd ever seen. Its length matched that of the sexual identity groups represented—lesbian, gay, bisexual, transgender, queer or questioning, intersex, or asexual (LGBTQIA). I could also see many service clubs, and probable heterosexuals with children, marching for their fellow citizens' rights. I had returned to Calgary, Alberta, home of the twice-elected, openly-gay, Muslim Mayor Naheed Nenshi, born in Toronto of South Asian parentage. I thought, *What great progress from my long-ago discussions with my gay drama friends at the University of Calgary in the 1960s.* I snapped a few photos with my phone and immediately sent some to one of them, Wes Tritter, in

249

LGBTQIA RIGHTS PARADE,
CALGARY, SEPTEMBER 2, 2017

Victoria, B.C., to inform him about my amazement with the now "open" city we'd left.

The previous day, I had flown from our new home in Albuquerque, New Mexico, to Calgary. I wanted to attend the memorial for David's twin brother, Alec, who had recently died of cancer. Alec and David, my double first cousins from Elmira days, had moved to Calgary in 1990. Like my father and his twin brother, they had worked together most of their lives. Their success in commercial real estate in downtown Calgary helped turn this "cowtown" into a modern metropolis of 1.3 million. David was the salesman and Alec the numbers man.

When I arrived in Calgary, I rented a car at the airport and drove to the University of Calgary's campus, ground zero for the determination of my life's journey. After receiving my B.A. in 1968, I had headed to the small town of Kota Belud, Sabah, Malaysia, to teach high school for two years under the auspices of

CUSO—a life-changing experience. I loved living and working in Borneo—a tropical island with a complex mix of cultures, languages, and religions. There, I also started an international career as a filmmaker and multimedia producer.

In 1972, I married Elizabeth Diemer, who went by the diminutive "Beth," an American woman I met in Tokyo in 1970. We lived in Canada, Malaysia, Bangladesh, Kenya, Uganda, the USA, Russia, and then finally back to the U.S. in 2007. Along the way, we had two great children—Derek and Ruth—and they shared in some of our overseas adventures. By the end of 2012, I had had enough of my career and started to write about my adventures. We moved to Albuquerque in 2015.

By the time I returned to Calgary, I was well into finishing my first memoir, *Finding Myself in Borneo: Sojourns in Sabah*. It describes, in depth, my two years as a volunteer teacher and my second two-year stint in Malaysia, with Beth, when I became a CUSO field staff officer, overseeing the program. It also covers some more recent return visits.

At the University of Calgary's campus, I first headed to Rundle Hall, the residence where I lived for my first year—an eight-story building with three wings of rooms. I found it on the map and walked in its general direction, but could hardly recognize it. In the 1960s, the residences and dining hall sat on the edge of a grassy plain. We could sometimes see the Rockies on the horizon. But now, tall trees and newer buildings obscure the view.

The day I visited, the semester had not yet begun, but I found the door to Rundle Hall open. I entered and took the elevator to the third floor. I couldn't recall on which floor I'd lived, but this somehow seemed right. When I got off the elevator, I found that almost everything looked much the same as I had left it half a century before: the bulletin boards, the flooring in the center hall, the carpeting running down the three hallways. I could see some differences in the lounge: modern but well-worn couches and chairs and the old black-and-white TV replaced by a large flat screen.

I then descended to basement level and down through a tunnel to the dining hall, passing by heating pipes, now colorfully painted. This tunnel saved us from Calgary's long cold winters—no coats needed when going for meals. I entered the dining hall where I spent many hours chatting with friends and looking at the mountains in the distance. In compensation for the now blocked view, it provided a modern menu, including a number of self-service options and a coffee bar.

As I continued my search, occasionally asking for directions, I located the building where I had attended most of my classes, the social sciences block. I found some newer buildings and even a hotel on campus with an up-scale restaurant. The Student Center had been expanded and updated with a food court and bars—a radical transformation. Alberta had been so conservative in the 1960s.

I saw two theaters on the campus map and after some searching and asking directions, I entered the older one, University Theatre, where I had acted. Every detail remained as I remembered it, including one of the green rooms where I dressed and put on my makeup. I couldn't get into the old apron-stage theater because

UNIVERSITY THEATRE, 2017

of an ongoing rehearsal, but a muffled sound of the actors' voices penetrated the doors, reminding me of my forced audition and surprise venture into drama, so long ago. The acting I did voluntarily, and my one and only playwrighting course, helped steer me away from psychology. Interacting with my gay student friends in this facility and "counseling" them, opened my mind to other realities and dimensions of human experience. All of these pieces fit together to prepare me for my departure for Borneo.

By that time, I'd also located Wasfi Youssef, my roommate during my first year at Calgary. A few years earlier, I had found a book online titled, *Building Your Own Home: A Step-by-Step Guide* by Wasfi Youssef,

Ph.D., published in 1988 by Wiley Publications in New York. I had skimmed through it, but because it was all about small-scale construction rather than reinforced concrete, I wondered if the author was really my old friend and I set the book aside to consider later.

After moving to Albuquerque, I did a few searches on the internet and found some telephone numbers. A man with an Egyptian accent answered one of them and I introduced myself.

Wasfi said, "Neill! Where are you? How did you find me?"

"Wasfi, did you write a book on building your own house?"

"Yes, that's me. I've been living in this house I built for more than 30 years."

"I have a copy. I'm not building a house, but I am writing my memoirs and I've written about you, and how you influenced my life."

We talked for a long time, catching up on each other's lives. Wasfi had moved to New York and became a successful engineer. He'd married Theresa, who also came from Egypt. Thus began the renewal of our friendship. Calgary had been the nexus of change for me to a more international focus, and Wasfi had been at its center.

Some cousins I had not seen in ages attended Alec's memorial party on September 4, where we traded stories of long ago. Alec had left behind his Malaysian-born wife, Lee, and I always enjoy talking to her about the second home country we have in common. Alec had requested that there be no funeral, not even a celebration of his life, but David and David's daughter, Sandra, decided they should at least hold a house party. No one delivered a eulogy. It was a great time to catch up on what had happened in their lives and in Western Canada since I left. We also talked about people who had passed away, like Alec and David's younger brother Richard, my "blood brother" cousin who had been sent to Vancouver to live with our Uncle John Neill, the professor at UBC, after Aunt Doreen was killed in that car crash in Elmira, mentioned in Chapter 6.

By then, I knew the full story. Richard's adopted sister, our mutual cousin Catharine, had written to me about his life: "Richard arrived by plane when he was 12 and I was 10. Right before he came, I was in a fight with some boys at the stables, where I had access to a horse. I warned them, 'Just you wait, I'm getting a big brother and he's going to beat the shit out of you guys!' Boy, did I get a shock when Richard came down the ramp from the plane in his navy blazer and tie. He barely came up to my shoulders. I turned to Dad later that day and said, 'I'm not going to take him down to the stables.' I remember being so disappointed again after offering to play catch with him. He was so timid that he ducked instead of catching the ball."

Catharine described Richard's childhood in Vancouver. I had thought of it as a complete switch to an upper middle-class life in the home of a university professor. But by her account, he had a normal upbringing—adjusting to having a sister and eating different food, playing with their dog Kerry, managing a paper route, which he excelled at just as he did in Elmira, and rebuilding an old car when he reached 16 years of age and could drive. She said her mother encouraged him to socialize with his peers, but usually failed.

I had heard a different story. I knew that Aunt Ona had been pretty uptight and controlling when she watched over Catharine and me in the backseat during their visit to Elmira in our adolescence. Some of the family said she suffered from neurosis and it was a huge shock for Richard to become her adopted son after moving from the freedom he had had in Elmira. His new parents never allowed his brothers to visit him in Vancouver—an unpredictable influence.

Catharine continued, "Richard had a photographic memory and was brilliant—skipped two grades. He did wonderfully at UBC in a maths-physics double honors program in the 1960s, getting 100 percent in almost anything he tried. He belonged to the Science Student Association and at their year-end party, someone spiked the punch with LSD and Richard had a bad trip. He'd tried acid before and was incensed at the poor quality that caused the unpredicted reaction. He wanted to know why and set out to research the purity of acid and what went wrong. He perfected his LSD by trying it out on himself, and then began selling it on the streets."

Catharine related the rest of the story to me, though I knew a good part of it. Aunt Ona died tragically in 1972 after battling depression for many years. Her mental illness had been deep-seated in trauma she experienced when she was repeatedly raped as a child. No wonder she was so overprotective and strict with Richard and Catharine.

I had met Richard on my way to Malaysia in 1968 and again in Montreal in 1971, when David and Alec lived there. He was trying to go straight and doing well in an engineering job. But when I saw him again in 1975 in Vancouver, he was hallucinating and had paranoid thoughts. He had gotten himself so deep into drugs that he screwed up his brain. A few months later, he set himself on fire with gasoline in a forest near Golden, B.C. But he must have had second thoughts for he managed to put out the flames and stumble to the nearby road in great pain. Someone took him to the hospital in Golden, where he died.

Would his life have been different and longer if his biological mother and father had not met their own tragic deaths and he had remained in Elmira? We can only speculate. By then I knew human life can take so many precarious and unpredictable turns.

On one visit to Elmira, I walked through Union Cemetery to see Richard's small marker near his parents' tombstone, put there by his brothers. From the cemetery hill, I looked down at Elmira's chemical factory, still operating in full thrust next to the streets where I had played in the 1950s. New buildings now block the view of the hill where I had seen those magic structures, which I imagined to be "Africa" as a child. The factory's old smokestack continues to poke out of the new pipes and tanks in defiance of change.

Many long-term residents of Elmira now know about the chemical factory's involvement in the making Agent Orange for the Vietnam War in the 1960s. One article published by Toronto's Globe & Mail on July 12, 2008, titled *'Last ghost' of the Vietnam War*, had made

CHEMICAL FACTORY IN ELMIRA

my hometown infamous, directly linking it to the horrendous health problems the Vietnamese and other Indochinese people suffered from as a result of their direct exposure to Agent Orange. As dioxin entered the food chain through crops, animals, and fish, thousands more people were afflicted.

In the early 1970s, the managers of the company decided to stop making Agent Orange when they realized the product was doing so much permanent damage. If you google "Agent Orange, Elmira, Ontario" many articles appear and I read them and found more, some very technical. I also contacted two of the original activists who called for a cleanup, and the company engineer who had been in charge of it. I couldn't determine whether the factory only made Agent Orange's components, 2,4-D and 2,4,5-T, or actually mixed it and shipped it directly to the U.S. Army—not that it matters much. At least the higher-ups in the company must have known where the chemicals were headed, even if they didn't know exactly how they would be employed and the end result. The company has changed its ownership and name a few times since the 1960s, and its original decision makers have all passed away.

Between 1989 and 1991, Elmira's deep water wells were shut down, due to contamination from an organic chemical called NDMA and substances with unappetizing names, such as cyclohexylamine, xylene, and styrene. I looked up NDMA, and found it to be a water-soluble carcinogen in experimental animals and a suspected carcinogen in humans, which comes from, among other processes, the manufacture of pesticides, rubber, alkylamines, and dyes.

A new source of water for the town—a pipeline from the City of Waterloo—was completed in 1991. The company's former environmental engineer wrote to inform me that Agent Orange's components—2,4-D and 2,4,5-T—weren't involved in the contamination of the town's water supply, but traces of the dioxin it produced, TCDD, can still be found in the soils around the factory and the creek. He further stated this compound isn't water soluble and therefore posed no danger. But another report I read claimed that TCDD would dissolve in water with the help of organic solvents, which the chemical company and other businesses have leaked into the creek and soil of the town over the years.

I continue to wonder about the long-lasting effects of 2,4-D and 2,4,5-T production, as well as DDT, the pesticide which had motivated Rachel Carson to write *Silent Spring* in 1962. By all accounts, Elmira's factory had stopped production of DDT in 1972, when it was banned. Surprisingly, I found an online video of an August 2015 news item by a local TV station, titled, "Elevated levels of DDT found along creek that feeds Grand River." It gave some details of the final report by the cleanup advisory committee, including the fact DDT and its breakdown components, DDD and DDE, remain in the sedimentary soil of the creek at more than 2,900 times higher than the Province of Ontario deems safe, and that the dioxin from the production of Agent Orange, TCDD, is also present with possible long-lasting effects on the environment.

I watched a recently-released video on Elmira's chemical woes: *Toxic Time Bomb*. This documentary gave me more details on the effects of the presence of the chemical factory in my hometown. I learned that, at one time, the company had actually been required to make plans for dealing with various levels of emergencies in case of accidental leaks of toxic substances into the air over Elmira. In those plans, our old house on Duke Street was in or very near the so-called "kill zone."

As I watched the video, my thoughts drifted back to playing in the creek's chemical soup as a kid and getting "buggered"—lost on islands in the spring floods—and seeing "frogs with two heads and fish with only one eye" during those long summers in the 1950s. I chuckled when I read a sign in the video, which the township had finally posted on the creek: "Consuming fish caught here may be hazardous to your health." No kidding!

I read details in the online report titled, *Elmira Water Woes: The Triumph of Corruption, Deceit, and Citizen Betrayal*. It portrayed a 30-year struggle between citizen activists, the chemical company, other polluters, Ontario's Ministry of Environment, and the other governmental bodies involved. Yes, some basic cleanup actions have been carried out, but those dangerous substances remain deeply embedded as silent evidence of past deeds.

All of this investigation led me to a kind of wonderment about how my brother and I, my cousins, and other generations of Elmira's children, had escaped illness or death from cancer. No long-term health impact studies have ever been carried out. I concluded that the company had been "left off the hook" from the start, for Old Order Mennonites own most of the farms located on the creek downstream from the factory, and the company probably calculated they would never undertake lawsuits, for the Old Order's main concern is with the court of judgment at Saint Peter's gate.

On visits home, my parents, my siblings, and most of the other people I met, never discussed these matters much. Long-term residents are proud that unlike many small towns in the industrial northeast of the U.S., Elmira never became a "rust belt" community. Many of the original downtown businesses and some of the factories remain today, and new ones have been added. The town, now with a population of about 12,000, also serves as a bedroom community for surrounding cities—busy and innovative places.

If I tried to discuss the possibility of cancer and other health issues from the town's former water supply, people would usually dismiss it as so much "media hype." In the early 1980s, Dad suffered from a serious form of cancer, but miraculously beat it through chemotherapy, love and care from the family, Mom's prayers, and possibly something I encouraged him to follow— visualization meditation, which involves patients using their own mental images of beating up cancer cells. He chose the only sport he was ever fond of, and pictured miniature boxing gloves punching the aberrant cells.

My family blamed Dad's cancer on long-term stress. He and his brother had lost control of their company in 1969. They started to import Claas Combines from Germany in the mid-60s—those machines I helped to assemble before leaving for university. This line of business proved to be a mistake for McKee Brothers and eventually it took the company down, or at least out of the hands of Dad and my uncle. At the time, these German combines had only been tested on the manicured terrain and crops of Europe, not the rough farmlands of North America with its heavy corn, and they kept breaking down. Eventually, McKee Brothers, under new ownership and management, went belly-up due to over-expansion—too many big ideas and new product lines.

Uncle Gerald wisely got out before this happened, and with the money from his shares he bought a metal fabrication business in Waterloo called Gil-Wal Machine. Dad remained general manager of McKee Brothers for a few months, but saw the writing on the wall, quit, and took his money out too. He came back on a salary as its product development manager for a few years, but then left again to buy into Gerald's company on a 50-50 basis. Neither of them wanted to "punch the clock" for others. They purchased a vacuum pump business from a Mennonite farmer-entrepreneur who had become overwhelmed by his success at making these devices for sucking up cows' milk on dairy farms, or any kind of sewage. This man's congregation didn't allow electricity, so he set up his workshop—precision metal working machines using hydraulic fluid driven by a diesel engine.

When Dad told me this story, I marveled at this Mennonite man's ingenuity in getting around religious doctrine. Dad also told me the man had a bad back— one of his reasons for selling a successful business. For short-term relief, the guy had purchased a massage chair and his more modern Mennonite neighbor threw an electric cord over the fence for his convenience. It could be tossed back when the deacon came to visit.

Next, Dad and Uncle Gerald purchased the old Link Belt Foundry in Elmira—one of the original polluters that had rained small black flakes of carbon on our town. They renamed it "Procast Foundries Inc." and installed a stainless-steel scrubber, bringing the smokestack emissions into environmental compliance. They also designed and installed a waterfall air purifier inside the building to greatly improve conditions for employees and decrease ground-level emissions. They moved Gil-Wal to Elmira, renaming it "Elmira Machine Industries." Among other products, this company machined and assembled the pump, with some parts made at Procast Foundries. But they kept their two businesses completely separate so they could track all transactions and carefully manage profit margins.

In the 1990s, Dad and Uncle Gerald made peace with

the brothers they had argued with over business deals in the 60s, and they held big family reunions again. Beth and I were happy to attend one in Elmira when on vacation from my work in Africa. Gerald and Dad retired in a comfortable manner, after selling the foundry to another investor and Elmira Machine Industries to my younger brother Philip, who had joined earlier, bringing with him his degree in business, new energy, and new ideas. As it turned out, he was the only one of us to display Dad's entrepreneurial drive and business skills. He expanded into new product lines and eventually brought in his three sons to work with him...and so, Elmira Machine Industries and McKee Farm Technologies Inc. continue in my hometown today.

In 1979, the work of my dad and Uncle Gerald was written up as a case study in *The Technical Entrepreneur, Inventions, Innovations & Business* by Donald S. Scott and Ronald M. Blair (eds.), published by Sanford Educational

GERALD AND RUSSELL MCKEE IN RETIREMENT

THE FINAL MCKEE HAYING SYSTEM - STACK N' MOVER

Press. In May of 2007, these two technical entrepre-
neurs were inducted into the "Waterloo Region Hall of
Fame" for their many achievements. Besides their more
recent successes, they had manufactured and sold more
than 10,000 McKee shredder harvesting systems. These,
plus their tractor-mounted snowblowers, livestock water
bowls, corn harvesting heads, chisel plows, and "Insta-
Hitch" were sold throughout North America, and even
on other continents.

In spite of Dad's preoccupation with his businesses,
he and Mom always took advantage of their "prodigal
son's" distant and exotic locations. In 1970, Dad and
Mom joined me in Borneo for a week, and also visited
me and my family in Bangladesh and Kenya in the
1990s. They had no fear of travel to less developed countries and I admired them for that. Dad wanted to visit
us in Russia too. As a child he had read a picture book
on the marvels of St. Petersburg and it had stuck in his

ALMA AND RUSSELL MCKEE VISITING BANGLADESH, 1991

memories. But he had become a little too frail for such travel when Beth and I lived in Moscow.

In the summer of 2007, immediately after we returned from Russia to our place in Maryland, I received a call from my brother Glen. My father, at age 87, had taken a fall. I cut short my vacation and headed to my hometown. On arrival at the hospital in Kitchener, I found Dad pretty agitated after many tests, which he always hated. My brothers and I met with the doctor who told us his heart was only pumping at about a third of normal capacity. A dizzy spell resulting from congestive heart failure had caused the tumble. Dad didn't want any more medical interventions. Decisions had to be made because my mother could no longer look after him in their retirement condo. Mom, always practical, posed the question, "Russell, do you want to go to a nursing home or your heavenly home?" He chose the latter.

A few hours later, I sat down to talk with Dad and Uncle Gerald, two inseparable souls in business and in life. As they reminisced about primary school days, the doctor approached my dad and asked, "Mr. McKee, I understand you don't want any more medical treatment for your condition. Is that correct?"

Dad turned to the doctor and said, "No sir, not for me. Let's wrap this up." Dad then looked toward Gerald and said, "Remember how we dealt with that bully at school, Cale Beatty..." and the conversation and chuckling continued.

For the next ten days, I stayed at my brother Philip's cottage on Conestoga Lake, formed from the valley where all the McKee children, including me, had played and hiked for a century and a half. I went into the hospital daily, catching up with Dad on the economy of Russia, its manufacturing and transition to capitalism, and the features of St. Petersburg. Every day I went down to the hospital cafeteria to fetch him a Tim Hortons coffee, which he loved. Visits to Tim Hortons coffee and donut chain had become part of Dad and Mom's routine, after Dad's retirement.

Some of the nightshift nurses were immigrants from Africa and he loved talking to them. They told me about Dad's stories of visiting me in Africa and Asia. These ladies reminded my dad of the poor conditions of the few black families near the farm where he was born. They descended from American escaped slaves and he raged against such injustice. They said tears came to his eyes as he reminisced.

As the days passed, I became his constant daytime caregiver and negotiator for higher levels of morphine.

I think it was easier for me to fulfill his wishes than my siblings, who lived nearby him most of their lives. They were more emotional about his passing. Over this period, the pauses between his sentences increased. He would drift away for a moment and then return. Gradually, his breathing deepened and he lost conscious contact completely.

The last morning of his life at sunrise, I watched a flock of Canada geese taking off from Conestoga Lake, right above the bridge, now deep under water, where Dad and his brothers, as well as Glen and I, had fished as boys. I knew it had to be the day. I hurried to the hospital to be with him. He was fading quickly, his breaths now far apart. After several hours, I took a break to get a Tim Hortons coffee and brought it back to Dad's room. A moment later, I saw and heard him take his last breath, a faint rattle, and he slipped away. I closed his eyelids. That instant our daughter Ruth called and we cried together. After the call, I stood beside him in solitude before alerting the medical staff and phoning my siblings and son. Soon, Mom arrived with Glen, and she sat with Dad by herself to say goodbye to her lifelong partner.

After Dad was gone, Mother lived for eight more years in an assisted living facility across the road from the apartment where our family first lived in Elmira—the place where the Mennonite lady warned her, when she brought me home from the hospital, that I wouldn't survive. Mom's eyesight had begun to fail in her mid-80s due to macular degeneration. For the last few years, she could only see shapes and colors, but she recognized the people she knew by their movements and voices.

Beginning in 2013, after retiring from my international career, I visited her quite often, driving up from Maryland. I had begun to study our family's genealogy and to gather stories for a book on family history, and we talked about that. She loved to go for drives with me, my family, or any friends who would take her. She could identify most of the familiar places of Elmira and environs by their shapes. As usual, she wanted to go to Tim Hortons for coffee and to chat about the family, as well as gossip about some of the wackier goings on in her retirement facility. She said the world in there was "too small."

Mom's name Alma means "nourishes the soul" in Latin, and in that she excelled for me and my siblings, as well as for many other people. She had to become a good planner, raising the six of us in three phases over so many years—my brother John arriving in 1966 when she was 46, after I had left home and was working at that iron ore mine in Wawa during the summer.

In April 2015, about a week before Mom died, brother Glen's wife, Marg, went to her residence to help her choose a dress for a family wedding shower. Mom had placed a blue dress in the middle of her closet and when Marg asked if it would be okay to set it aside, the answer she got was, "No, that's my funeral dress, you leave it right there."

On the day of her death, she went to her exercise class, as usual, got her hair done for the shower, and made plans to play a card game called "Aggravation" with her friends in the afternoon—she couldn't actually see the details of the cards, but her companions helped her—a very cooperative group in spite of the name of their game.

While eating lunch, she felt some discomfort in her chest and headed upstairs to her room to lie down and take her usual afternoon nap. Shortly afterwards, like Dad, she passed away from congestive heart failure. She died with little fuss, the same way she had lived.

Beth and I were still living in Maryland when we heard the news, and we drove up to Elmira for the funeral. I had the honor of delivering a eulogy for Mom in the church hall, and attending a celebration of her life in the very same church basement, where I had been elected president of Young People's Group in 1964. It was like closing the circle.

Mom often said that she was "Scottish, Irish, Dutch, Yankee, and Canadian." I knew the Scots-Irish Canadian side but not much about the Yankee and Dutch side— her mother and grandmother from Wisconsin. By the time Mom passed away, I had begun to gather stories, digging deeper into the lives and circumstances of my Canadian and American ancestors. And that's the subject of my travel memoir: *Guns and Gods in My Genes: A 15,000-mile North American search through four centuries of history, to the Mayflower.*

So, in my 70s, I'm still a "kid on the go!"

About the Author

Neill McKee is a creative nonfiction writer based in Albuquerque, New Mexico. His first travel memoir, *Finding Myself in Borneo: Sojourns in Sabah* has won three awards. His second travel memoir, *Guns and Gods in My Genes: A 15,000-mile North American search through four centuries of history, to the Mayflower*, is a deep dive into his ancestry, written in a refreshingly creative way. McKee holds a bachelor's degree from the University of Calgary and a master's degree in Communication from Florida State University. He worked internationally for

45 years, becoming an expert in the field of communication for social change. He directed and produced a number of award-winning documentary films and videos, popular multimedia initiatives, and has written numerous articles and books in the field of development communication. During his international career, McKee was employed by Canadian University Service Overseas (CUSO); Canada's International Development Research Centre (IDRC); UNICEF in Asia and Africa; Johns Hopkins University, Baltimore, Maryland; the Academy for Educational Development and FHI 360, Washington, D.C. He worked and lived in Malaysia, Bangladesh, Kenya, Uganda, and Russia for a total of 18 years and traveled to over 80 countries on short-term assignments. In 2015, he settled in New Mexico, using his varied experiences, memories, and imagination in creative writing.

www.NeillMcKeeAuthor.com

NeillMcKeeAuthor@gmail.com